WILDLIFE OF THE WORLD

6

Honeyguide – Komodo dragon

Marshall Cavendish

New York • London • Toronto • Sydney

Published by Marshall Cavendish Corporation
2415 Jerusalem Avenue
North Bellmore, New York 11710 USA

Wildlife of the World
    p.   cm.
    Includes bibliographical references and index.
    Summary: Alphabetically-arranged articles introduce over 300 animals, describing their habitat, behavior, and efforts to protect them.
    ISBN 1-85435-592-9 (set)
    1. Animals—Juvenile literature.
[1. Animals—Encyclopedias.]
I. Marshall Cavendish Corporation.
QL49.W539   1994
591—dc20   93-3581
                   CIP
                   AC

Printed in Malaysia by Times Offset (M) Sdn Bhn
Bound in the United States by Lake Book Manufacturing

Produced by Brown Packaging

Editorial Consultant	Dr. Joshua Ginsberg
Editor	Deborah Evans
Assistant Editor	Amanda Harman
Art Direction	Sandra Horth
Design	Alison Gardner
Photo Research	Amanda Baker
Illustrations	John Francis

Marshall Cavendish

Editorial Director	Evelyn Fazio
Development Editor	MaryLee Knowlton

PICTURE CREDITS

The publishers would like to thank NHPA, Ardingly, Sussex, for supplying the following pictures:

ANT 378,379; Henry Ausloos 331,372; Anthony Bannister 340,341,342,343, 354,355,362; J Blossom 332; Dave Currey 330,Stephen Dalton 326,348,374; Manfred Danegger 328; Nigel Dennis 324,325,350,353; RJ Erwin 366,367, 368,370; GDT 345,358; Helio & Van Ingen 329,369; Tony Howard 364; EA Janes 335,347; Rich Kirchner 361; Stephen Krasemann 337,356,360; Gerard Lacz 333,359,380,381; Tsuneo Nakamura 339; Haroldo Palo 352,377; Peter Parks 363; WS Paton 349; Peter Pickford 351; Ivan Polunin 334; Otto Rogge 365; Jany Sauvenet 336,346; Philippa Scott 382,383; John Shaw 357; Eric Soder 344; Morten Strange 327,376; R Thwaites 338; Barbara Todd 373; Alan Williams 371.

Additional pictures supplied by:
Frank Lane Picture Agency 375.

Front cover: Koala, photographed by Gerard Lacz.
Title page: Scarlet ibises, photographed by Jany Sauvanet.

STATUS

In the Key Facts on the species described in this publication, you will find details of the name, appearance, breeding habits, and so on. The Status of an animal indicates how common it is.

Extinct	No sighting in the last 40 years
Endangered	In danger of becoming extinct (following the U.S. Fish and Wildlife Service list of Endangered and Threatened Wildlife)
Threatened	A species that will become endangered if its present condition in the wild continues to deteriorate (following the U.S. Fish and Wildlife Service list)
Rare	Not threatened, but not frequently found in the wild
In captivity	A species that is extinct in the wild, but has been kept successfully in captivity
Feral	Animals that have been domesticated and have escaped into the wild
Common	Frequently found within its range, which may be limited
Widespread	Commonly found in many parts of the world

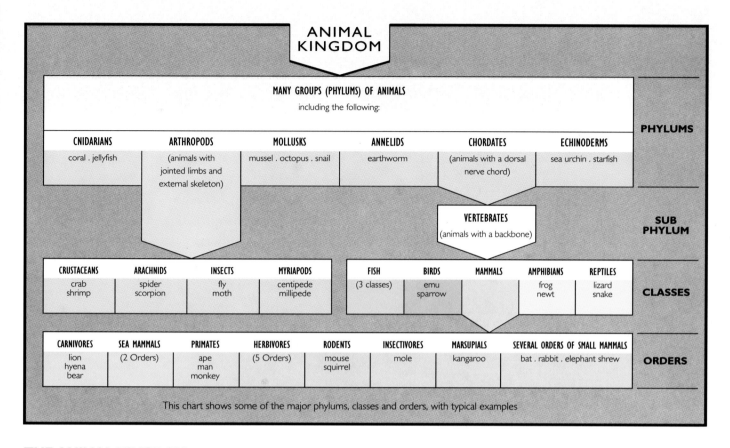

This chart shows some of the major phylums, classes and orders, with typical examples

							PHYLUMS
MANY GROUPS (PHYLUMS) OF ANIMALS including the following:							
CNIDARIANS coral . jellyfish	**ARTHROPODS** (animals with jointed limbs and external skeleton)	**MOLLUSKS** mussel . octopus . snail	**ANNELIDS** earthworm	**CHORDATES** (animals with a dorsal nerve chord)	**ECHINODERMS** sea urchin . starfish		

VERTEBRATES (animals with a backbone) — SUB PHYLUM

									CLASSES
CRUSTACEANS crab shrimp	**ARACHNIDS** spider scorpion	**INSECTS** fly moth	**MYRIAPODS** centipede millipede	**FISH** (3 classes)	**BIRDS** emu sparrow	**MAMMALS**	**AMPHIBIANS** frog newt	**REPTILES** lizard snake	

								ORDERS
CARNIVORES lion hyena bear	**SEA MAMMALS** (2 Orders)	**PRIMATES** ape man monkey	**HERBIVORES** (5 Orders)	**RODENTS** mouse squirrel	**INSECTIVORES** mole	**MARSUPIALS** kangaroo	**SEVERAL ORDERS OF SMALL MAMMALS** bat . rabbit . elephant shrew	

THE ANIMAL KINGDOM

In the eighteenth century, a botanist from Sweden called Carl von Linńe (often known by his "Latin" name, Carolus Linneaus) outlined a system of classifying plants and animals. This became the basis for classification all over the world. Scientists use Latin names so that all animals (and plants) can be identified clearly, even though they have different common names in different places.

Linneaus divided living organisms into two kingdoms: plants and animals. The animal kingdom (*above*) is divided into many phylums. Most of the phylums of the animal kingdom contain strange creatures — microscopic animals, sponges, coral, jellyfish, slugs and insects — without the backbone and central nervous system that we associate with the more familiar animals. Each phylum has further divisions, known as classes. For example, vertebrates (animals with backbones) are a subdivision of a phylum, and are divided up into several classes: mammals, birds, reptiles, amphibians and three types of fish.

Each of these classes is broken down further into different orders. The mammal class, for instance, includes carnivores (meat eaters), insectivores (insect eaters), various hoofed mammals, primates (monkeys, apes), rodents (rats, mice), marsupials (kangaroos, koalas), and so on.

In this publication, we give Latin names for genus and species for clarity and accuracy, but there are no detailed descriptions of the orders and classes. There is more information on the different groups of animals in Volume 13.

COLOR GUIDE

INVERTEBRATES

FISH

AMPHIBIANS & REPTILES

BIRDS

MAMMALS

In this publication the animal kingdom is divided into five different groups.

Honeyguide

Honeyguides are dull colored, small birds that live in quite remote parts of Africa, southern Asia, and Malaysia. They live in forests and open woodlands – and are never far from bees.

Guiding call

Insects form the major part of the diet of most small birds, but the honeyguide is unique in that it also eats the grubs of bees and the wax comb of beehives. It is the behavior of the Greater honeyguide that explains how this group of birds got its name. Wild African bees build their nests in hollow trees or clefts in rocks. The Greater honeyguide cannot get into the hive by itself because its bill is slender and delicate. When a honeyguide spots a bees' nest, it goes off in search of someone who can open it up. It attracts the attention of a Honey badger or a human (both are great honey lovers) with a persistent, chattering call. When it has caught their attention, it flies in short bursts toward the bees' nest, checking to see that it is being followed.

Once it reaches the nest, the honeyguide sits patiently and waits while the human

▼ *Perched on the decayed tree trunk that a swarm of bees chose for its hive, this Greater honeyguide is enjoying a feast.*

KEY FACTS

● **Name**
Greater honeyguide (*Indicator indicator*)

● **Range**
Africa south of Sahara

● **Habitat**
Woodlands and savannah

● **Appearance**
8 in (20 cm); drab gray-brown plumage with a yellow flash at the top of the wing; a pinkish beak

● **Food**
Insects, beeswax, larval bees

● **Breeding**
Breeds Sept-Jan; the female visits the male at a song post where they mate; the female lays one white egg in the nests of birds that breed in banks and holes in trees; the adult may damage the eggs of the host when she lays; nestlings have bill hooks that are used to lacerate the host's nestlings; the host incubates and raises the honeyguide's young

● **Status**
Widespread

or Honey badger takes down the nest to get at the honey. When it is working with a Honey badger, the Honey badger eats what it wants and leaves the indigestible honeycomb. However, a human "helper" usually takes the comb away to drain it and eat it. Among the tribespeople, tradition demands that a person should leave the bird at least part of the honeycomb, spiked on a twig or put in some other prominent place.

Learning without teachers

How the honeyguide learned to do this, and how the people and Honey badgers learned to follow, is a mystery. The Scaly-throated honeyguide (*Indicator variegatus*) behaves like the Greater honeyguide in calling helpers to a hive.

When there's honey about, the honeyguide seems a friendly little bird. But at breeding time its behavior towards

other birds is not so friendly. Like the North American cowbird and the European cuckoo, the honeyguide is lazy about nesting. It never builds its own nest, but lays its eggs in the nests of other birds. It selects a host that nests in banks and holes in trees, such as the Little bee-eater or Red-billed wood hoopoe.

When they hatch, the honeyguides throw the other birds out of their nest or attack them with a sharp hook on the tip of their beaks. The host bird then has to rear the young honeyguide until it is ready to fly off alone. It is thought all 17 species of honeyguide breed in this way.

It has been shown in laboratory tests that young honeyguides eat wax and bees' grubs from a very early age, without ever being taught. Scientists have not been able to find any reason why these particular grubs and the wax are such an important part of the diet. The young honeyguides, once they have left the nest, develop the characteristic call that attracts humans or Honey badgers to beehives without ever hearing it from their parents.

▲ *Other species of honeyguide, including the Lesser honeyguide shown here, still enjoy wax, grubs, and honey from the comb, but do not guide mammals to the site to help them get at the hive.*

NATURAL HABITAT

Greater honeyguide

See also **Honey badger**

Hornbill

As their name implies, hornbills are famous for their large bills, which often have serrated cutting edges like knives for cutting up food. Most species live in lush forests in Africa and Asia, but some of the African species live in drier savannah grassland habitats.

Big beaks

In many species of hornbill, the large bill is crowned by what is known as a casque. This may be a narrow, bony ridge that reinforces the upper bill, but in some species it is a much more elaborate structure, a sort of tube that may be larger than the bill itself. This gives the bill a very heavy look, but it is actually extremely light. Both males and females have casques, but they are usually larger and more elaborate in the males. Scientists are not quite sure about the casque's purpose: in the Great and Rhinoceros hornbills, it is used in fighting or to knock down fruit; it may be used in recognizing

KEY FACTS

● **Name**
Red-billed hornbill (*Tockus erythro-rhynchus*)

● **Range**
Africa, apart from north Africa

● **Habitat**
Scrub and open woodlands

● **Appearance**
20 in (50 cm); mainly white or gray, with black markings on the wings and tail; strong downwardly curved red bill

● **Food**
Insects and fruit

● **Breeding**
Nest holes usually 45-90 ft (15-30 m) above ground in a tall forest tree; the female shuts herself in and incubates the eggs for 30-45 days; the male feeds the female and the young

● **Status**
Rare

◄ *The Red-billed hornbill of Africa has a characteristic downward-curving bill.*

the age, sex, and species of an individual; and it may amplify the hornbill's song.

Hornbills are particularly noisy birds, giving high-pitched cries and whistles, usually with their heads raised so that their bills point upward. One species makes ever louder and faster hoots until it breaks into a maniacal laugh — a characteristic sound of the Asian rainforests. Hornbills also make loud whirring noises as they fly and flap their wings. They are usually seen in pairs or in small groups, though larger numbers may congregate at a tree when the fruit is ripe. Apart from the species that live on the ground, hornbills sleep in roosts in tall trees for much of the year: 100 have been counted at a single roost.

Sealed nests

The nesting habits of the majority of hornbills are unique. The pair select a suitable hole — in a hollow tree, or

▲ *This Rhinoceros hornbill shows off his huge casque (the top part of his bill). He is supplying his mate and young with food because they are sealed into a nest in a hollow tree. He will take away food remains and droppings so the nest stays clean.*

sometimes a cave-like crevice in the rock. After mating, the female seals herself into the hole, using material supplied by the male (usually earth mixed with sticky mucus). She pats this into the entrance hole until she is sealed in, with only a narrow slit left open. The male brings food to the nest and passes it to the female (and later the nestlings). In some species the male continues to feed the female and her young until the young are ready to leave the nest. In other species the female breaks out when the chicks are about half grown and helps with the work of feeding them. The chicks then reseal the nest and only break out when they are ready to fly. This habit protects the young from predators.

NATURAL HABITAT

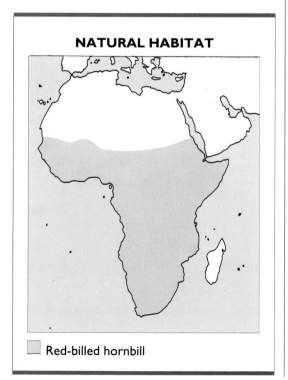

☐ Red-billed hornbill

Hornet

Hornets are well known: they are generally thought of as insects to be avoided, as these large wasps have very nasty stings. If you see a hornet buzzing around, leave it to buzz off: if you try to swat it and follow it, it is likely to lead you back to its nest. And if you disturb a hornets' nest, you may be swamped by hundreds of worker hornets who will chase you away, stinging as they go.

Although a single sting from a hornet is not usually a problem, multiple stings may cause terrible reactions. These wasps are responsible for several deaths each year in the United States. Occasionally, people have a serious allergic reaction to a hornet sting, and this can be fatal if the right drugs are not given very quickly.

Nests of paper

Hornets are part of the family of *Vespidae*. All the wasps in this family live in large social groups and are able to make a kind of paper to construct their delicate nests. Favorite sites for hornets' nests are under the eaves of outbuildings or in trees. As long as they are left alone, the hornets keep busy building the nest and feeding their grubs, but if they are disturbed they become very aggressive. In the swamps of

▲ *The hornet, like other members of the wasp family, has a distinctive narrow "waist" between the thorax and the abdomen, which gives rise to the description "wasp-waisted" for someone with a very slim waistline.*

Florida, they often build their nests on branches that hang down over the water; as the swamps were opened up for tourism, many "explorers" found themselves crashing into the nests before they had even noticed them.

Hornets build a new nest each year. The process starts in the spring, when queen hornets come out of hibernation. A queen hornet finds a site and then starts to build a nest. She uses plant material and wood from trees and fences. First she scrapes away some of the material, and then she mashes it up with her mandibles (jaws), moistening it with saliva. She builds a small, papery bell, open at the lower end, and in the middle she makes a layer of cells. To start with there are only a few cells, which the queen fills with eggs. When they hatch, she has to feed them.

After a month, the grubs have grown so large that they fill their cells. They seal themselves in and pupate. A week later, the first grubs emerge as adults. The first to emerge are always workers, which are female. They help to feed the larvae and continue to build the nest until there are several layers of cells encased in an outer covering of paper. The whole structure takes on the shape of a football. Now the queen can devote all her time to laying eggs. As the workers emerge, the queen goes back and refills each cell.

Special diet

During this time the adult hornets feed on carbohydrates – sweet and sugary foods from flowers and fruit. This gives them a lot of energy for traveling large distances in search of food. However, the grubs need a high protein diet for rapid growth, so they are fed on insects.

Toward the end of the summer, some of the cells are fed on slightly different diets to create new queens, and some unfertilized eggs that are laid become male hornets. In the fall the new queens and males emerge and fly together. The queens are fertilized and then hibernate. In the spring the whole process starts again.

KEY FACTS

● **Name**
Hornet (*Vespa* and *Vespula* species)

● **Range**
All continents except Antarctica

● **Habitat**
Temperate and subtropical woodlands, gardens, and outbuildings

● **Appearance**
Up to 1½ in (4 cm); brown and yellow bands around the abdomen; the wings folded when at rest

● **Food**
Adults eat fruit and nectar; the larvae are fed on insects

● **Breeding**
Queen fertilized in the fall and carries sperm through hibernation; she builds the nest and lays eggs in the spring

● **Status**
Widespread

◀ *The hornets' cells are hexagonal (six-sided) tubes that fit together with no gaps between. The white coverings are created when the grubs are pupating.*

See also **Bee, Wasp**

Horse

A stampede of wild horses, with the sound of hoofs pounding across the plains, is one of the most powerful images of the Wild West that one can think of. It therefore comes as a surprise to many people to find that there is now no such thing as a wild horse. All populations of

▼ *These mustangs, found on the western plains in the U.S., are descended from horses that were brought to America by Spanish settlers 400 years ago.*

modern day "wild" horses came about as a result of domestic horses escaping or being released back into the wild. In fact, when Europeans first arrived in the New World in the sixteenth century, there were no horses in either North or South America at all. Spanish colonizers brought the species to America in the late 1500s.

However, fossils show that horses or their relatives once did exist in North America. They disappeared from the North American plains 8000 years ago, soon after humans came to the continent. Sixty million years earlier, a small five-toed creature the size of a large dog lived in the North American forests. This animal, whose name *Eohippus* means "dawn horse," was the first horse species. Fossils of horses in various shapes and sizes have been found. About five million years ago, there were eight or ten species of horse in North America alone, and the family had spread throughout Asia and into Africa.

Small ancestors

Early horses were small, slow, short-legged creatures with three or five toes formed into imperfect hoofs. They lived in the forests where they found a variety of fruit, nuts, leaves, and other plant material to eat. As time went by, horses got larger and faster. Their diet shifted from feeding on bushes to grazing on grass.

The modern horse is large and graceful. It has a single "toe" or hoof and long legs that allow it to run rapidly across the grasslands to escape from predators. All

▶ *These white horses live wild in the Carmargue in France.*

KEY FACTS

• **Name**
Domestic horse
(*Equus caballus*)

• **Range**
North and South
America, Australia

• **Habitat**
Open plains, open
woodlands, wherever
grass is plentiful

• **Appearance**
Males and females
are approximately
the same size,
measuring up to
6½ ft (2 m) from
head to rump, and
weighing up to 1100
lb (500 kg) in most
species; enormous
color variation, with
white, brown, and
black being the most
common colors

• **Food**
Mainly grasses, herbs,
and reeds, but will
also eat tender young
leaves

• **Breeding**
Females are usually
seasonal, giving birth
in the spring, 11
months after mating

• **Status**
Common

six species of modern horses, zebras, and asses are really very similar to one another. Scientists put them all in the same group, *Equus,* which means that they share a common ancestor – probably a plains-living horse that lived about two million years ago.

Useful to humans

Horses were domesticated in Mongolia about 5000 years ago. Ever since then they have been extremely important to humans, and have been used for tasks such as pulling plows and carts. Swift-footed horses provided people with the only fast form of land transportation until the invention of trains and cars. Horses also provide meat and leather. And in some areas they even supply their owners with milk. Indeed, the horse is probably among the most adaptable of all the animals that humans have domesticated.

Since horses were domesticated, a wide variety of breeds have been developed. Professional breeders look for particular characteristics such as speed and gracefulness in the case of racehorses, or strength and power in the case of large farm horses. Many different kinds of pony have been bred, too.

Ponies are generally smaller and stockier than other horses, with thicker coats and longer manes. Some tiny ponies, such as British Dartmoor ponies, were bred specifically so that they were small enough to work in coal mines. The smallest horse in the world is the Falabella horse from Argentina. It grows to about 3 ft (93 cm).

Return to the wild

Horses that were once domesticated and released or escaped into the wild are called feral. Horses have been set free to roam the wild in many places, and feral

horses can be found in the West Indies, in the deserts of the southwestern states, the high altitude plains of the Rocky Mountains, the deserts of Australia, and the pampas or plains of South America.

One of the things that makes horses so adaptable is their diet. Unlike cows and antelopes that need fine, green grass to survive, they are able to eat many kinds of grass – even the coarse, dry variety. They are also able to process food much more quickly than bovids (cow-like animals). So when only poor quality food is available, bovids die because they can't digest it, while horses thrive by just eating more and pushing the food faster through their digestive systems.

Social beasts

Most of what we know about the social behavior of wild horses is taken from scientists' observations of feral horses, such as Przewalski's horse, which has been bred in captivity to be released into the wild again.

Horses live in family groups called harems, which are made up of one male

▲ *During the nineteenth century, the only truly wild horse was found on the Mongolian plains of central Asia. It was originally "discovered" by a Polish explorer named Przewalski and has since been called Przewalski's horse (shown above). Soon after their discovery, Przewalski's horses became extinct in the wild. Only now, after decades of captive breeding, are Przewalski's horses being brought back to Mongolia to roam wild again.*

and up to five females. Each of these harems have their own home ranges and they are tight and stable family units. They never split up, moving from their winter territories to their summer grazing areas as one unit.

In most parts of the world, horses are very seasonal breeders, and the young are born soon after the spring begins. Horses are able to breed again almost immediately after giving birth. A female horse (mare) will only mate with the male (stallion) in her family group. Because horses have an 11-month gestation period (the time when the baby is growing inside its mother), the young are born at about the same time every year.

Leaving the family group

Young horses (foals) stay in their family groups for a fairly long period of time compared to many other animals. Males leave their family groups when they are 18-24 months old and join up with other young nonbreeding males (colts) in bachelor groups.

The membership of these groups is extremely stable; the young males only leave the group when they are old enough

NATURAL HABITAT

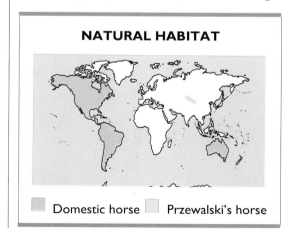

Domestic horse   Przewalski's horse

KEY FACTS

● **Name**
Przewalski's horse
(*Equus przewalskii*)

● **Range**
Central Mongolia

● **Habitat**
Grasslands and high
altitude semideserts

● **Appearance**
A sturdy horse,
measuring up to 7 ft
(2.1 m) from head to
rump, and weighing
800 lb (350 kg); dun-
colored flanks and
yellowish-white
underparts; the mane
is stiff and erect and
a deep, dark brown;
a large head, and
short, dark legs

● **Food**
Mainly grasses

● **Breeding**
Similar to the
domestic horse

● **Status**
Extinct in the wild;
feral populations are
endangered

▶ *Although she will be weaned at about 13 months, this young foal will stay with her mother until she is 16-18 months old. Then she will be ready to leave her family group.*

to start their own harem, or to fight a stallion for control of an existing one.

Young females (fillies) leave their family groups when they are 16-18 months old. At this time they are ready to breed and produce their own foals. Young fillies will frequently join an existing harem but they never stay in the harem in which they were born. By doing this, horses avoid inbreeding.

Scientists who study the domestication of wild animals often wonder why some animals tame very easily and others can never be domesticated. One thing that may make horses so easy to domesticate is they way they organize their social life. All horses leave the family group in which they are born, so they are used to being moved out of a social group. Yet all horses join new groups and are very loyal to the members of this group even though they are not closely related. This loyalty to other members of a group may explain why horses are so loyal to their owners.

Unknown forest horses of Europe
Until the late Middle ages, approximately 800 years ago, a rare and strange horse called the tarpan lived in European forests. Scientists believe that the extinction of the tarpan may have been caused by humans. The forests were cut down to make way for farmland, and the horses were probably killed for their meat and hides.

We know very little about the tarpan, except that it existed in Europe for thousands of years. Tarpans or other wild horses are commonly found in the cave paintings of southern France and were used by early humans as a source of food. Scientists think that tarpans may have been the same species as Przewalski's and domestic horses, but their extinction means we will never know for sure.

See also **Ass, Zebra**

Horseshoe crab

▲ These Malaysian Horseshoe crabs have been turned over so that you can see their bodies tucked inside their horseshoe-shaped shells.

In the days before the dinosaurs walked the earth, and even before there were any plants growing on the land, the seas were dominated by little creatures called trilobites – creatures that lived between 570 and 225 million years ago. We know about these creatures from fossils: they had horny shells, and were the first animals to have eyes. Trilobites are now extinct: their only living relative is the Horseshoe crab, which has lived, in much the same form as it is today, for over 300 million years.

Not a true crab

The Horseshoe crab is a strange looking creature, quite different to the true crabs.

It has a similar hard shell, but all its limbs are tucked underneath the shell.

The Horseshoe crab shuffles its way along the bottom of the sea, looking for food such as worms and small clams. It is able to crush shellfish with its spiny limbs, then it tucks them into its mouth, which is also beneath the shell. It uses its tail to steer itself along: the back part of its shell forms a hinged, rectangular section that extends to a sharp pointed tail. There are short spines around the base of the tail, which form part of the Horseshoe crab's defenses. Its eyes, high on top of its shell, are always on the lookout for both predators and prey.

Coastal breeding

Apart from its long history, the Horseshoe crab is remarkable for its breeding habits. While land crabs migrate to the water to lay their eggs, Horseshoe crabs migrate to the shore at breeding time. Every spring, along the North Atlantic coast, when there is a full moon and a high tide, hundreds of thousands of Horseshoe crabs drag themselves up the beaches. They are only seen for about three nights each year. The females arrive first, followed by the smaller males, who cling to likely mates in their eagerness to breed.

The females half bury themselves in the sand, ensuring that the eggs they lay are covered. This helps to protect the eggs from sea birds and other predators. Soon after the females have laid their eggs, the males shed their sperm over them to fertilize them. Then the eggs are left with a protective covering as the Horseshoe crabs return to the ocean. It is a month before the eggs hatch. When they hatch

there is another high tide and full moon, so the water reaches the eggs and the young can swim out to sea. The larvae are quite different from the adult Horseshoe crabs and very similar to the trilobites of 500 million years ago. Before they reach adulthood they will grow and shed several shells.

▲ *During the mating season, Horseshoe crabs allow themselves to be washed ashore. They look like huge cobblestones washed up on the beaches of the east coast.*

NATURAL HABITAT

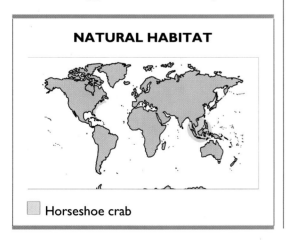

☐ Horseshoe crab

Hummingbird

Hummingbirds are among the most delightful creatures in the bird world. Most are tiny; indeed one hummingbird is the smallest known bird in the world: at $2\frac{1}{4}$ in (6 cm) long, the Cuban Bee Hummingbird (*Mellisuga helenae*) actually has a body about the size of a large bee. The largest, the Giant hummingbird from the Andes of South America, is $8\frac{1}{2}$ in (22 cm) long. Hummingbirds are also beautifully colored and are a remarkable sight flashing through forests, woodlands, or gardens with brilliant, light-reflecting feathers. There are over 300 species of hummingbird, all of which come from North, Central, or South America.

Sweet feeders

Hummingbirds are perfectly adapted for feeding on the nectar of flowers. They beat their wings rapidly so that they can hover while feeding and reach their needle-like bills inside flowers. Inside their bills, they have a long, tube-like tongue

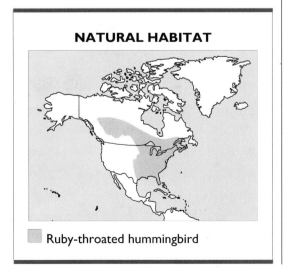

NATURAL HABITAT

Ruby-throated hummingbird

▲ *Rufous-breasted hermit hummingbirds, like most species, show a preference for red flowers. Some flowers depend on these little birds for pollination. If flowers and their natural habitat are destroyed, the birds cannot survive.*

that they can extend to lick up the nectar. Different species have bills of different lengths and shapes adapted to take nectar from the flowers that they visit. For example, the Andean sword-billed hummingbird (*Ensifera ensifera*) has a probing beak that is 4 in (10 cm) long – almost as long as its body. It feeds from deep-throated flowers. The flowers benefit from this nectar-gathering activity because the hummingbirds pick up pollen on their breasts as they feed, and the pollen fertilizes the next flower they visit.

As they move between the flowers, hummingbirds are like living helicopters with swift darting flight, sudden stops and starts in midair, and the ability to hover, fly backward, shift sideways, and fly straight up and down. Many of these skills are unique to hummingbirds. Studies of one particular species showed that when hovering, its wings beat at 55 beats per second, and when flying this went up to 75 beats per second. At such speeds you can hear the distinctive hum that gives these birds their name.

All this activity takes its toll: they have to feed almost continuously to stay alive because of the amount of energy they use in flying and because of their small size.

Breeding patterns

In most species of hummingbird, the male is more brightly colored than the female. The breeding season and courtship start when there is plenty of nectar; since most species of hummingbird feed on particular flowers, their breeding is timed to coincide with the flowering period. The males (and sometimes the females) establish feeding territories, chasing away large bees and moths that may invade. They guard their favorite flowers with swooping flights above them, and this same flight is used to attract females.

At the same time the males puff up their throat feathers; most males have jewel-like feathers around their throats called "gorgets." A male and female only spend a short time together, often mating in midair. Then the female gets busy building a nest and establishing a nesting territory,

driving males out of her area. The nest is often elaborate, compactly built of soft plant down and young leaves. The female fastens the structure in position on a branch with her bill, using silk from a spider's web. Then she decorates it with lichen and moss until it is like a small knot about the size of a walnut.

Keeping up numbers

Twenty-one different hummingbirds have been observed in the US, but only eight are found north of Texas. The Ruby-throated hummingbird is the only member of the family that is regularly seen in the eastern states. In the west, the Rufous hummingbird is the most common, summering further north than any other hummingbird. Again, it travels south to Mexico for the winter. Although no species are listed as endangered, all hummingbirds are protected: during the nineteenth century, thousands of them were caught and stuffed and used as ornaments.

KEY FACTS

● **Name**
Ruby-throated hummingbird (*Archilochus colubris*)

● **Range**
Eastern N. America; winters in Panama

● **Habitat**
Flowers, gardens, wood edges

● **Appearance**
3-3³/₄ in (8-9 cm); the male has a red throat, shiny green back, gray front, and forked tail; the female lacks the red throat and has a blunt tail

● **Food**
Feeds on nectar from a great variety of flowers; also eats many insects

● **Breeding**
In woods, forests, orchards; 2 eggs are laid March-July, incubated for about 16 days; the young fly at 20-22 days old; 2-3 broods per year

● **Status**
Common, protected

◄ *The Ruby-throated hummingbird visits the eastern states in the summer and flies some 500 miles south over the Gulf in the winter.*

Humpback whale

The Humpback whale is perhaps one of the most distinctive whales in the world. It is extremely agile and acrobatic, with a playful nature. Despite its huge size, it is often seen leaping high into the air above the surface of the sea.

The Humpback whale has a massive head and a huge, streamlined body. The snout is covered with prominent bumps or tubercles. It is unique among whales in having long flippers measuring up to 17 ft (5 m) in the adult – almost a third of its total body length! Indeed, the name of the group to which the humpback

▲ Humpback whales are very acrobatic. They enjoy breaching – leaping right out of the water and diving back in again. No one really knows why they do this. Some people suggest it is male aggressive behavior during the mating season, but it could be just for the sheer enjoyment of leaping!

belongs, *Megaptera*, means "great wing" in Latin. And when it prepares to dive below the surface of the sea, it makes a kind of "hump" shape with its back, giving it the common name of humpback.

Filter feeders

Humpbacks generally eat microscopic shrimp-like organisms called krill, or small schooling fishes such as sardines, mackerel, and anchovies. They catch them by "lunging" with their huge mouths gaping.

The Humpback whale, like the Blue whale, is a rorqual. Rorquals are whales that do not have teeth, but instead have large baleen plates in their upper jaws (270-400 in the humpback) that "sieve" out food from the surrounding water. These special filtering plates are edged with bristles, and the longest may be up to 40 in (1 m) long. When the whale "catches" a mouthful, the water is expelled through the gaps in the baleen, leaving the food sticking to the plates.

The humpback's method of feeding requires huge amounts of food to be present at once. In order to stop the schools of fish and "clouds" of krill from dispersing, the humpback may surround its prey with a circle of bubbles that it releases from its mouth or the blowhole on top of its head.

To catch the maximum amount of food that it needs to survive, the humpback also has about 20 large grooves extending from its throat to its belly that allow its mouth to stretch enormously.

NATURAL HABITAT

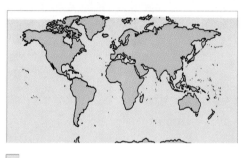

Humpback whale

Traveling through the oceans

Humpback whales are migratory, spending the warm summer months feeding in cold polar oceans and traveling many hundreds of miles to warm tropical waters to breed in the winter. Unlike other rorquals, Humpback whales swim very close to the coastline during this seasonal migration. They are sociable animals, and it is common to see small family groups with three or four individuals (or even as many as 10) swimming and feeding together.

Humpbacks are also very vocal and can often be heard communicating or "singing." These "songs" are like those of birds, with repeated phrases and patterns. They are also very loud and may be detected by humans with special listening equipment over 100 miles (160 km) away.

Once they have reached their winter breeding grounds, the humpbacks stop feeding and the males spend all their time competing with each other for the right to mate. Now they can be extremely aggressive, and as well as singing to attract the females they fight, lunging at each other and hitting out with their fins. Some lift their heads from the water as they do so, opening their mouths as wide as possible to seem larger and more threatening, and slapping their tail flukes and pectoral flippers on top of the water with huge, resounding splashes.

▼ *During the winter, when the whales reach their breeding grounds in warm, tropical waters, a single calf is born. This "youngster," swimming with its mother, weighed about 2000 lb (900 kg) at birth and measured up to 15 ft (4.5 m).*

KEY FACTS

- **Name**
  Humpback whale
  (*Megaptera novaeangliae*)

- **Range**
  All oceans, to the edge of ice packs

- **Habitat**
  Deep waters near coasts; migrating from polar oceans in summer to tropical waters in the winter

- **Appearance**
  Large, streamlined body, gray-black in color and measuring up to 50 ft (15 m); a massive, rounded head and long pectoral flippers, growing up to 17 ft (5 m) long; the whole body is covered in small tubercles, and there are about 20 throat grooves stretching from the throat down to the belly

- **Food**
  Krill, crustaceans, small schooling fishes

- **Breeding**
  A single calf is born during the winter in the warm, tropical breeding grounds; it feeds on its mother's milk for 12 months

- **Status**
  Endangered

See also **Blue whale**

Hyena

Hyenas have a bad reputation. They are often considered to be scavengers, stealing food from other predators such as lions, cheetahs, or wild dogs. Although hyenas do steal carcasses, they kill the vast majority of the food they eat. Not only are they efficient killers, but to a hyena, a wasted scrap is unheard of. Their coats are mottled beige and brown, providing good cover in the dry grasslands. In the case of the Spotted hyena, the markings are irregularly sized blotches, whereas other species are predominantly striped.

Hunters in the dark

Hunting mainly at night, hyenas are extremely flexible in their hunting strategies. When large prey are rare they will hunt smaller gazelles, rodents, tortoises, or pangolins. But they are extremely skilled in hunting in groups and can take down animals as large as buffalo, zebras, small rhinoceroses, or young hippos. They use their characteristic call,

▲ *The hunched shoulders of a hyena give it a rather sulky look. Its great strength is in these shoulders, where the muscle creates a high, arched back.*

a long whooping sound, to keep in contact during a hunt. Well-organized packs of hyenas even challenge lions for their prey. They have little to fear from large cats or other predators that live in the same area.

Hyenas have evolved to make the most of their kills. Their jaws are lined with flat, square, strong back teeth, capable of crushing bones and sharp enough to rip tendon and sinew. The muscles that run from their forehead to their jaws (the *maseeter* and *temporalis* muscles) are enormous, providing tremendous force to the jaw. Their jaws are so strong that they have been known to eat tires off a parked car! Their digestive systems are also extremely efficient and dissolve most of what they eat — including fur and bone.

Females first

Hyenas live in large, extended families called clans, with up to 50 animals sharing a denning area. Unlike most animals, female hyenas are larger than males, and females dominate males in all aspects of social life. The social life of the hyena is highly structured, with families of sisters, aunts, and female cousins all living in the clan. Each adult female produces two or three young each year and related females will often help rear each other's young. The young are nursed for up to eight months — unusually long for a carnivore.

Female hyenas look like males. Before they are born, baby hyenas are exposed to very high doses of chemicals normally only present in males: the male hormone, testosterone. This results in female sexual organs that look almost exactly like those of males. These high doses of testosterone also result in very aggressive young.

Tough cubs

Baby hyenas are born with their canines or "dog teeth." Scientists knew that the young hyenas lived only on milk and did not need teeth for eating, and for many years they thought they used their teeth to defend themselves. The real story is much more gruesome. Within the hyena clan, dominance is determined by size. Size, in turn, is determined by how much food a baby gets from its mother. If a young hyena kills a littermate, it gets more food, grows bigger, and is dominant in the clan. The teeth hyenas are born with, and the agressive nature they get from large doses of male hormones, enable the young hyenas to kill their weaker littermates.

▲ *Young hyenas stay with their mother for several months after birth, and her milk is the mainstay of their diet for about 8 months.*

Such behavior is seen in many birds, but is extremely unusual in mammals.

Hyenas are feared by people, but attacks by hyenas on humans are extremely rare. Occasionally, hyenas kill sheep and cattle, but such events are not as common as some people think. Hyenas can be beneficial as they are natural garbage disposers, scavenging dead animals and garbage in areas around human habitation. Nonetheless, many countries still have active campaigns against hyenas. Because they will so readily scavenge a dead carcass, poisoning is an effective and deadly way to eliminate hyenas.

In addition to the Spotted hyena, there are two other species, the Brown and the Striped hyenas. Both are nocturnal. The Brown hyena is found only in the deserts and woodlands of southern Africa. Mainly a scavenger, it also eats small mammals, birds, fruit, and insects. The Striped hyena was once found in southern Europe but now only exists in North Africa, the Middle East, and parts of India.

NATURAL HABITAT

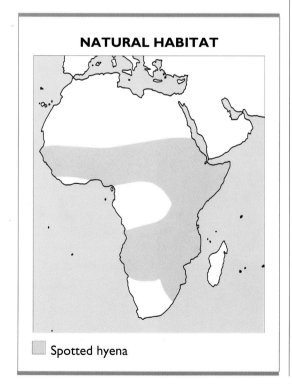

☐ Spotted hyena

KEY FACTS

● **Name**
Spotted hyena
(*Crocuta crocuta*)

● **Range**
Savannah belt of western and central Africa, throughout eastern and parts of southern Africa

● **Habitat**
Open plains and woodlands, but not true forests

● **Appearance**
A dog-like face with small, rounded ears and a large forehead; strong muscles in the shoulders; short hind legs that make the back slope downward; a distinctive spotted coat, brown on a beige background

● **Food**
Freshly killed hoofed mammals, but also scavenges and steals kills from others

● **Breeding**
Live in large, female-dominated clans; each female produces 1-3 young a year after a gestation of nearly 4 months

● **Status**
Common in some areas, but widely persecuted through poisoning campaigns

See also **African wild dog**

Hyrax

Hanging in a small tree or bush, or scampering over the rocky outcrops of central and southern Africa, hyraxes look very much like large rodents, perhaps squirrels. Their long, chunky bodies, small heads and ears, and their constantly growing front teeth are also rodent-like. Given these similarities, it often comes as a surprise to people that the closest relative of the hyrax is, in fact, the elephant! Elephants, dugongs, and hyraxes all shared an ancestor some 60 million years ago. Since then, of course, they have all developed in quite different ways.

The relatively close family links with elephants and other hoofed animals, although not obvious from their size, are seen in the way hyraxes breed. Although adult hyraxes weigh under 10 lb (4.5 kg), they have a gestation period that is seven months – more than double what one would expect. When the young are born they are very highly developed, but their mothers continue to nurse them for up to five months. For comparison, this would be like a woman being pregnant for 20 months and breastfeeding for three years.

Rock lovers

The best known of the hyraxes are the four species of rock hyraxes, also known as dassies. Rock hyraxes all share a similar

▼ *These Cape rock hyraxes seem to have few predators on the rocky coastal shore. They huddle together for warmth in the evening sun.*

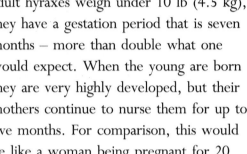

KEY FACTS

● **Name**
Cape rock hyrax or dassie
(*Procavia capensis*)

● **Range**
Most of Africa and into Asia

● **Habitat**
Almost any rocky habitat, from deserts to mountains, including coasts

● **Appearance**
17-18 in (43-46 cm) long; a tube-shaped body, short neck and a small head with small ears; the sharp and curling front teeth look like those of a porcupine; short, coarse hair which varies in color with location, from black to light brown

● **Food**
Fine green grass, berries, fruit, leaves

● **Breeding**
Extremely long (7 month) gestation period; each female produces 1 to 4 young each year, nursing them for 4-5 months

● **Status**
Common

social system. They live in unusually large social groups with up to five to seven females and their young, a dominant or territorial male, and sometimes young nonbreeding males. Each female raises her own young, although the females join together to protect the young from predators. At about 18 months, males leave the territory in which they are born and move to new groups. Because the rocky areas in which they live are often far apart, many young males die during the move. Like many primate species, young females stay in the group in which they were born for their entire lives.

Scent marking

Hyraxes will vigorously defend their territories from intruders, although such active defense is rarely needed. Using oil glands on their hindquarters, hyraxes mark their territorial boundaries with a strong

smelling musky oil. These marks tell any creature that enters the territory that a rock pile is already occupied.

Scent glands may also serve to bond a hyrax group together. In the night, when the hyraxes are sleeping, they often come together in dark holes or cracks in the rock and pile up one on top of another in a heap. Other animals, including pet gerbils, also do this.

Two explanations have been given for this heaping behavior. The first is very straightforward. Although hyraxes live in Africa, the nights can be very cold indeed, with temperatures as low as 30 or 40°F (0-8°C). By piling up together, the hyraxes keep warm. The piles, however, also result in each hyrax rubbing up against other hyraxes and exchanging scent, perhaps to make a communal smell that identifies the group.

▲ *If a hyrax feels threatened by a predator (or a photographer!) it will bare its teeth and growl in much the same way as a dog. However, these creatures are much smaller than dogs and look rather like large rabbits with short ears.*

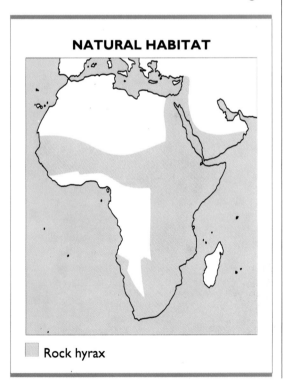

NATURAL HABITAT

Rock hyrax

Ibex

▲ These bucks are competing for mates during the breeding season, using their huge horns as powerful battle weapons while others look on.

The ibex is a large mountain goat that is found on the highest mountaintops, above the tree line where little else survives. Like other mountain goats, it is successful because it is able to specialize in a habitat so severe and inhospitable that almost no other animal can compete with it.

Keeping warm

The ibex has adapted well to this extreme environment. Its shaggy brown coat acts as insulation, keeping the ibex warm even in sub-zero temperatures. Its hoofs, like those of many mountain goats, can support the entire animal as it picks its way across the rock face. Its diet is varied, and it eats almost any vegetation that it can find — roots, shoots, leaves, and grass are all eaten and digested efficiently.

In the summer months, food on the mountaintops is plentiful, but when the winter arrives with heavy snow, the ibex must work harder for its dinner. In some areas, ibex scamper along windswept cliffs, finding grass and shrubs exposed by the wind. However, in other areas, they use their feet to dig the buried food out from under the snow. Their sense of smell is keen — the ibex will dig away up to a foot (30 cm) of snow if it detects buried acorns, a rich source of energy in the frozen landscape.

Competition for mates among ibex is severe. This competition has led to three

KEY FACTS

● **Name**
Ibex (*Capra ibex*)

● **Range**
Mongolia and central China, through Afghanistan, the Arabian peninsula, and south to northern Ethiopia

● **Habitat**
High altitude meadows and rocky outcrops above the timberline (the highest altitude at which trees occur)

● **Appearance**
A majestic beast, measuring up to 5 ft (1.5 m) and weighing as much as 240 lb (110 kg); massive, thick horns arching over its head; an even, dark brown coat; a small "beard" on the chin

● **Food**
Grasses, reeds, and the leaves of shrubs

● **Breeding**
Intense competition among males for mates; females bear a single young 5 months after mating

● **Status**
Rare in some areas

▶ *After mating is over, large male ibex stay with a herd of females. Indeed, this behavior is more common in goats than in their close cousins, the sheep. The group structure of ibex is very flexible, with animals leaving and joining herds as they search the mountaintops for food. Ibex, unlike many animals, do not have territories that they defend from competitors, but wander widely and freely, with larger males using their size to defend the females in their herd rather than a territory.*

distinctive characteristics in male ibex: a large body, large horns, and incredibly nimble feet. When females are ready to breed, males try to defend them. The larger the male, the more aggressive he becomes during the breeding season.

A large, dominant male will chase smaller males across the slippery slopes and rocky crags of the high mountains, physically removing them from their breeding areas. When large competitors show up, however, males must engage in dangerous battles. Two large males charge each other, slamming their heads and horns together in a massive clash. These fights can lead to death but, more often than not, the losing male turns around and sticks his rump in the victor's face, a clear sign of submission in many animals.

Owned by humans?

Humans have domesticated many goat-like animals. In fact, the origins of our domestic goats are uncertain, and some scientists think they may have come about as a mix of several wild species. For years no one thought that the independent and mountain loving ibex could ever have been domesticated by humans. The discovery of ancient hieroglyphics or rock carvings has changed this theory. It seems that thousands of years ago, the ancient Egyptians captured and kept ibex. These animals may have been used as farm animals, or they may just have been kept in ancient zoos – no one is certain.

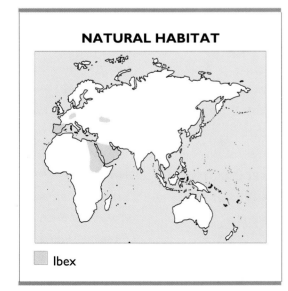

NATURAL HABITAT

☐ Ibex

See also **Goat**

Ibis

The ibis is a bird with a long history. The Ancient Egyptians worshipped the Sacred ibis (*Threskiornis aethiopicus*), which was believed to be the animal form of Thoth, the god of wisdom and magic. Ibises were often mummified and buried in temples with their pharaohs. In Egypt the Sacred ibis has now been extinct for nearly 100 years, but it is still common in Africa south of the Sahara.

Ibises are elegant wading birds, with sleek feathers and long legs, and they seem to enjoy each other's company as well as the company of other birds. There are some 27 different species of ibis thoughout the world, all living in tropical and warm temperate zones.

Flocking to water

Most ibises live and feed in shallow freshwater lakes, marshes, and swamps:

▲ Scarlet ibises are a startling sight, perched in the treetops in large groups. They are native to South America, but are accidental visitors to southern Florida and the Texas coast. The first ibises to nest in the states (the White, White-faced, and Glossy ibises) arrived at the end of the nineteenth century and have successfully moved northward.

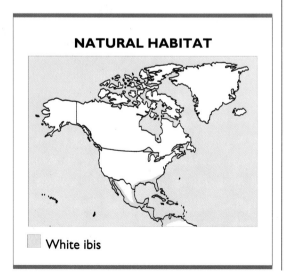

NATURAL HABITAT

☐ White ibis

KEY FACTS

● **Name**
White ibis
(*Eudocimus albus*)

● **Range**
South Carolina to
Texas, Mexico,
Central America,
parts of Caribbean

● **Habitat**
Marshes and swamps

● **Appearance**
22-24 in (55-58 cm)
mainly white with
red legs; bill is red,
downward-curving

● **Food**
Invertebrates:
insects, crustaceans

● **Breeding**
In colonies, usually
with herons and
other large waders;
the nest is built by
both parents and is a
platform of sticks in
trees, especially
mangroves; 3-4 eggs
are laid March-Aug
and incubated for 21
days by both parents;
the chicks are fed
regurgitated food

● **Status**
Common

▶ *The White ibis is
becoming more
common in eastern
North America where
it is protected by law.*

they are found on flooded farmland and in some parts of the world they move onto the rice fields. They have long legs and downward-curving beaks that are perfect for stalking through the water and probing the bottom for food. Ibises also have partly webbed toes to help spread their weight as they stalk through the mud.

Rather than use their eyesight to catch their prey, they use their beaks to probe for it, catching small crustaceans, fish, and insects, as well as larvae and frogs. Ibises that live away from water catch beetles, ants, grasshoppers, reptiles, and sometimes eat carrion, eggs, or even small rodents.

Nesting time

Ibises can be seen in large groups, feeding together and making grunting calls to each other as they feed. At breeding time they form colonies, often mixing with other species of wading birds. The birds pair up each season, working together to build an untidy nest of sticks and twigs. Most ibises choose low trees near wetlands, but sometimes they nest on cliffs and rocky outcrops. Some species build their nests on the ground. There is often a display at the nesting site, with pairs of birds bowing and stretching their necks forward.

Both male and female care for the eggs: there are usually between two and five, and they have to be tended for nearly a month. After hatching, it is a month before the nestlings learn the strong flight techniques of their parents; it is three years before they are regarded as adults.

The numbers of ibises have dropped in many parts of the world, and two species, the Japanese crested ibis and Northern bald ibis, are endangered. All species of ibis found in North America (either permanent residents or occasional visitors) are protected by law.

Iguana

◄ *The Common iguana of Central and South America has leathery skin and spines down its back.*

NATURAL HABITAT

Marine iguana

Iguanas are a large family of lizards, most of which live in North, Central, and South America and the outlying islands. Members of the iguana family are also found in Madagascar and Fiji. There are over 600 different species of iguana altogether, of which 17 species or subspecies are threatened or endangered.

The species that are in greatest danger of dying out are those that live on islands. For millions of years, these species were able to live peacefully because there were few mammals to trouble them. However, in the Caribbean and in Fiji, the introduction of the mongoose, as well as domestic dogs, cats, goats, and cattle, have restricted the numbers of iguanas.

The Common iguana of northern South and Central America is a tree-dwelling

KEY FACTS

● **Name**
Marine iguana
(*Amblyrhynchus cristatus*)

● **Range**
Galapagos Islands

● **Habitat**
Coastal rocks

● **Appearance**
4-5 ft (1.3-1.7 m) long; red, brown, and black tortoiseshell effect; darker legs, spines over the head and backbone; a long tail; five toes on each foot, with claws

● **Food**
Seaweed and algae

● **Breeding**
Males defend the territory and fight for the females; the female lays 2 or 3 eggs in a sandy hole; the young often stay together for defense

● **Status**
Rare

lizard that lives near water. It is the giant of the family; it may grow up to 6½ ft (2 m) long. It is green in color with black rings on its tail and spines all down its back. It has been introduced into the southern states, particularly Florida. Although they are not meat eaters, they will fight other animals if they are attacked and can be quite fierce.

Seaside lizards

The most individual member of the iguana family is the Marine iguana. This creature is found only on the Galapagos Islands, on the equator off the coast of Ecuador. The Marine iguana is the only lizard that goes into salty seawater: it feeds on seaweed and algae. The sea gives it a plentiful supply of water, but in order to cope with the salty seawater it has special glands that remove excess salt from its food. It sprays this salt out through its nose with a cloud of tiny water droplets.

Once in the water, the Marine iguana either swims or walks on the bottom. It cannot breathe under water, but its heart rate slows down so that it can stay under the surface for a long time. As it swims, it uses its tail to propel itself through the water, and it uses its feet to steer.

Male Marine iguanas become territorial at the start of the mating season, fighting with other males. The fight is more of a ritual than an all-out battle, with head butting and clawing but no serious injuries. Once a fight is over, the intruder does not usually come back to fight again but retires to find another territory. The larger males establish the largest territories and mate with more females.

After mating, the female digs a shallow hole in the sand on the beach and lays two or three eggs. The ground is warm and the eggs well enough protected for them to be left to incubate without any attention from the mother, and they hatch after some three or four months. After hatching, Marine iguanas (and many other species of iguana) often live in groups with one acting as leader. If the mother has a second brood, the newly hatched lizards may form a group with the older ones, all on the lookout for predators.

Other species

Besides the huge Common and Marine iguanas, there are many smaller species that are found in North America. The Eastern fence lizard (*Sceloporus undulatus*) is found down the east coast, from Virginia to Florida, and across to Mexico. The spiny Texas horned lizard (*Phrynosoma cornutum*), with its flattened, armor-plated body, is found from Kansas to Texas and Arizona. The Chuckwalla (*Souromalus obesus*) is a desert species found in Nevada, Southern California, Utah, Arizona, and Mexico.

▼ *Young Marine iguanas usually form well-organized groups. They have been seen to groom and rub against each other and may huddle together for protection at night.*

Impala

Throughout southern and eastern Africa, in many habitats, one of the most frequently seen antelopes is the impala. The impala is an exceptionally graceful and beautiful animal. With long legs and a short, compact body, this medium-sized antelope is like an art student's study in color. It starts with a band of rich reddish-brown across the back and top of the flanks, followed by a creamy coffee color across the flanks and face, and ends in a pure or creamy white belly. Only the male impala have horns. The horns grow larger with age, starting first as spikes and, in subsequent years, growing longer until they arch over the head in graceful curves.

▲ A male impala drinks from a pool of water in the warm evening light; its elegant horns add to the graceful silhouette of this antelope.

Water in the diet

Impala are not found everywhere and they avoid both dense forests where no grass can grow and open plains with little bush cover. Where they are found, however, they are often extremely common. This is due, in part, to their broad tastes in food. Most hoofed animals, or ungulates, eat either grass (grazers) or bushes and trees (browsers). The impala is a jack-of-all-

NATURAL HABITAT

Impala

KEY FACTS

● **Name**
Impala
(*Aepyceros melampus*)

● **Range**
Eastern and southern
Africa

● **Habitat**
Open savannah,
woodlands, and bush,
particularly along
rivers

● **Appearance**
3$\frac{1}{2}$-5 ft (1.1-1.5 m)
long, 33-39 in
(77-100 cm) at the
shoulder; the males
are approximately 40
percent larger than
the females; the back
and upper flanks of
the impala are a
reddish-brown, fading
to pure or creamy
white on the
underside; a black
flash runs on both
sides, along the edge
of the rump and
down the thighs; only
the males have horns

● **Food**
Grass, fresh leaves,
fruits, seeds

● **Breeding**
Each female usually
produces only one
lamb per year, at the
start of the rainy
season; gestation
6-6$\frac{1}{2}$ months

● **Status**
Common

trades and will eat any green vegetation it can find. Impala must drink every day, so a source of drinking water is essential in their habitat.

Breeding in the impala is fast and furious. Most births in southern African impala occur just before the rains in May and June, about 6$\frac{1}{2}$ months after mating. Before the breeding season, large dominant males set up breeding territories, roaring to attract up to 20 females and to repel competitors. Because the breeding season is so intense and short, males stop eating during this time.

Plentiful and tasty

The strict season for breeding and births has developed for two reasons. The first is to take advantage of the green grass that sprouts with the first of the rains. The second and perhaps most important reason is that impala are the favorite food of many predators. Leopards, cheetahs, African wild dogs, jackals, lions, even baboons find young impala a tasty treat — easy to catch and delicious. If the young

▲ *When alarmed, impala flee through grass and scrub with an amazingly high, bounding stride. Their main enemies are big cats and wild dogs.*

were born throughout the year, the predators would pick them off one by one when they were most vulnerable. By giving birth all at the same time, the impala "flood" the predators with food. Even if they eat as much as they can catch, the predators cannot make a dent in the huge population of young impala. By the time the young impala lambs are five or six months old, many young have avoided being eaten and are larger and much harder to catch.

Three subspecies have been identified: the southern race (*Aepyceros melampus melampus*) in southern Congo, south to Zimbabwe and South Africa, and west to Botswana; *A. m. rendilis*, in northern Kenya, Uganda, and Tanzania; and the Angolan impala, *A. m. petersi*, also known as the Black-faced impala. The Black-faced impala may be threatened due to its relatively restricted distribution.

Jacana

▲ *The Northern jacana has a long slim body and long legs that are well adapted to its habitat of reeds and grasses along the water's edge. Here it spends its days searching for insects to eat and occasionally catching small or larval fish.*

Jacanas are small waders that look rather like gallinules, or moorhens. Their most striking characteristic is the length of their toes and claws, which enables them to walk on top of floating plants. The way that they walk on the leaves of water lilies gives them the nickname "Lily-trotter." Most have a fleshy shield above the bill, similar to that of a coot. Jacanas are generally more colorful than Common coots and American gallinules: they have feathers in tones of cinnamon, yellow, white, and dark brown or black.

Jacanas are found in many parts of the world: in marshlands, rice fields, along rivers, and near freshwater lakes in tropical and semitropical regions. There

are eight species altogether, of which only one is found in North America. This is the Northern Jacana that lives in Central America and occasionally ventures into Texas and the southern states.

They eat a mixed diet of insects (particularly those that live in water), mollusks, and the occasional small fish. They also eat the seeds of reeds and other water plants.

Tropical trotters

As they search for their food they stalk nimbly from leaf to leaf, occasionally jumping a patch of water with the help of a flick of their wings. As they land, they have the habit of raising their wings so that they almost meet over their backs. This movement shows off the paler colored feathers under the wings and the spurs (like sharp claws) on the leading edge of their wings. These spurs are used to defend their territories during the breeding season. It is possible to approach

NATURAL HABITAT

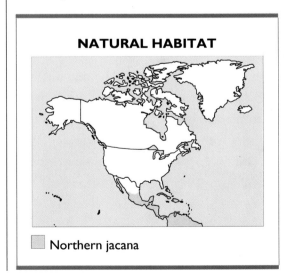

☐ Northern jacana

jacanas quite closely without alarming them. However, if they are frightened by a large bird or other animal, they stand motionless and become very difficult to see amongst the reeds in spite of their quite strong coloring.

Role reversal

The breeding season for most jacanas is during the wettest part of the year when insects are plentiful. The Northern jacana, which lives mainly in Central America, lays its eggs between April and August in most parts of Mexico, or between January and October in Costa Rica.

The most remarkable feature of the jacana is its unusual breeding pattern. The female jacana (which is larger than the male) usually establishes a territory. Within that territory there may be three or four males with whom she mates. The males are the nest builders and, after the female has laid her eggs, the males look after the eggs and rear the young. The nest itself is a mass of floating twigs and leaves, and sometimes it drifts over ponds and swamps.

Once the eggs have hatched, the male feeds and protects the chicks. In heavy rains the male takes the chicks under its wing to provide shelter. The chicks take three or four months to develop enough to leave the protection of their father. The female is thought to visit her mate regularly in the breeding season.

▼ *Jacanas are found in tropical and subtropical regions. This African jacana has strong blue coloring on the front of its head. It is the male that builds the floating nest and tends the eggs.*

KEY FACTS

● Name
Northern (or American) jacana (*Jacana spinosa*)

● Range
Central America and the Caribbean; a rare visitor to Texas

● Habitat
Aquatic habitats

● Appearance
8-9 in (20-22 cm) long; the female is larger than the male; a yellow bill, a forehead with a red and yellow frontal shield; the head, neck, chest, and upper back are glossy black, elsewhere is a deep chestnut or maroon; greenish-yellow flight feathers

● Food
Mainly insects; some small fish

● Breeding
Female has the territory with 1-4 smaller males; the nest is built by the male; green leaves on a floating mat of plants, built up to stop the eggs from rolling out; usually 4, almost round eggs; the male incubates them for 22-24 days

● Status
Widespread

See also **Coot, Crane, Gallinule**

Jackal

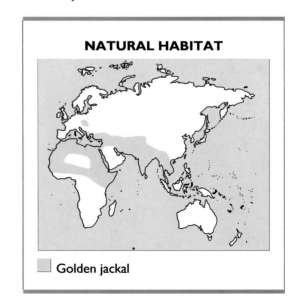

◄ *The Black-backed jackal of southwestern Africa is a small jackal with distinctive black and silver fur covering its back. The male defends its territory fiercely against other males, while females try to chase away any female intruders. Young jackals may stay with their parents for several years, playing and having mock battles with each other, until they are old enough to leave the family group.*

There are only four species of jackal, yet jackals are at the same time among the most common and among the rarest animals in the world. The Black-backed (or Silver-backed) jackal is common in the plains and woodlands of eastern and southern Africa. The Golden jackal, found in Africa and east Asia, is also common and expanding its range. The Side-striped jackal, with a white stripe on its side, is common in central and southern Africa. Yet the Simien jackal is becoming very rare. Found only in the highland mountain meadows of Ethiopia, perhaps only 350 of these elegant brown-backed, white-bellied, large dog-like animals remain. Disease, habitat loss, and years of war have all contributed to the near loss of this species.

Not so nasty

Jackals, like their cousins the foxes, dogs, and other wolf-like animals, are often looked upon with distaste. They are thought to be scavengers of dead, rotting carcasses, or carriers of fatal diseases like rabies. To call someone a jackal is not a compliment but an insult. Yet jackals are harmless and very playful animals, good parents, and keen hunters. Although

NATURAL HABITAT

◻ Golden jackal

they sometimes try to steal meat off the carcass of an animal killed by a lion or hyena, most of their diet consists of seeds, fruit, insects, and small mammals. Jackals are particularly fond of mice and rats, and one pair of jackals can eat hundreds, if not thousands, of cane rats in a year. Not surprisingly, jackals play an important part in maintaining the natural balance in many parts of Africa, helping to keep rodent pest numbers low.

Puppy love

Male, or dog, jackals usually pair up with a female, known as a bitch. This family group lives on a small territory of around 110-550 acres (0.5-2.5 km²). The breeding season varies by species, but is often timed to coincide with the time of year in which food is plentiful. Two

months after mating, three or four puppies are born to the family pair. The puppies remain underground in a den for three or four weeks. The den is a safe shelter from the weather and, more importantly, from predators such as eagles, hawks, hyenas, and lions.

The pups are fed on milk by the mother for a short time, approximately eight to ten weeks, and then move on to solid food. Males provide at least half the food for the puppies. The pups reach sexual maturity in the year following their birth. In years when there are too many jackals in an area, however, the young pups do not breed until they are two years old.

▼ *This Golden jackal lives on the grassy plains of the Serengeti National Park in Africa. The jackal is increasing its range and has been seen in Italy.*

KEY FACTS

- **Name**
  Golden jackal
  (*Canis aureus*)

- **Range**
  Widely distributed in East and North Africa, southeast Europe, south Asia to Thailand

- **Habitat**
  Usually in open grasslands and scrub; also found near human habitation

- **Appearance**
  4 ft (1.3 m) long excluding tail; pale golden brown fur, or yellow with darker brown tips; relatively short hair; a long, black-tipped tail

- **Food**
  Omnivorous: seeds, fruit, insects, beetles, lizards, birds, and particularly small rodents; also eats dead animals and hunts the young of small antelopes

- **Breeding**
  Usually form stable pairs; groups of up to 20 animals are found if food is plentiful; otherwise they form smaller groups, with one-year-olds helping to raise the pups

- **Status**
  Common

Jack rabbit

◄ *As you can see from this picture, jack rabbits have huge ears. There are lots of blood vessels very close to the surface skin of these ears, which give out heat so that the animal can keep cool in its hot, dry habitat.*

The jack rabbit is the fastest of all the rabbits and hares in the world and can run at speeds of over 45 mph (72 km/h). It is found in the grasslands and deserts of western North America and Mexico. Four species are found in the United States: the White-tailed, the Black-tailed, the White-sided, and the Antelope jack rabbits. Like their close relative the Snowshoe rabbit, these jack rabbits are not rabbits at all, but are in fact hares. They have much longer hind legs than rabbits and generally longer ears, too.

Quick and watchful

With large ears and long hind legs, the jack rabbit has adapted well to a life spent on open ground, where it can be spotted easily by predators and other enemies.

The jack rabbit has excellent hearing, so it can detect the sound of a predator from a considerable distance. It often stands up on its hind legs on the lookout for danger. When it feels threatened it either lies very still and low on the ground or it bolts, running and jumping at great speed, sometimes bounding in long jumps of up to 20 ft (6 m). Every so often the jack rabbit jumps up to get a view above the surrounding vegetation — sometimes up to 5 ft (1.5 m) high.

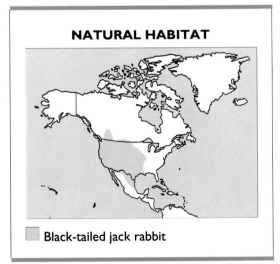

NATURAL HABITAT

Black-tailed jack rabbit

The soles of the jack rabbit's feet are covered with thick hairs, which help to keep a grip on the ground and so allow it to run faster and jump further. However, when the jack rabbit is fleeing from danger it does not rely totally on speed. It also tries to escape pursuit by "jinking" – suddenly turning and changing direction. Apart from human hunters its main enemies are coyotes and eagles.

A day in the life of a jack rabbit

During the day, jack rabbits lie up in shallow hollows known as forms, which they make among grasses and other vegetation. They may have several forms scattered around their home range, some of them temporary but many of them permanent and used by generation after generation of jack rabbits.

Like other hares, three of the four species of jack rabbit do not make burrows. The exception is the Black-tailed jack rabbit, which digs a short burrow where it can escape from the heat of the sun's rays in the summer.

Once evening comes, jack rabbits leave their forms or burrows to look for food. They feed mainly on grasses and other plants such as snakeweed and sagebrush. Those jack rabbits that live in dry regions also feed on mesquite and cacti when the grass has dried up. They have developed a unique method for eating a prickly cactus. First they chew around the spiny area. Then, when this becomes loose, they pull it out to reveal the moist edible flesh that lies underneath.

Jack rabbits breed from one to seven times a year, depending on where they live and other factors such as the weather. As the breeding season begins the males will chase each other around and fight violently, usually biting and kicking out at each other with their back legs. Injuries to one or both fighters can occur, but in the end one of the pair will usually withdraw by running off.

Leverets

The female builds a nest among vegetation on open ground and she lines the nest with fur that she removes from her breast. The litter may consist of one to eight young (called leverets) although three or four is the usual number. The leverets are covered with fur at birth and their eyes are open. They can also move about a little as soon as they are born, although they remain in the nest until they are about four weeks old.

KEY FACTS

● **Name**
Black-tailedjjack rabbit or Jackass hare (*Lepus californicus*)

● **Range**
Mexico, western U.S.

● **Habitat**
Grasslands, farms, deserts, semideserts

● **Appearance**
Head and body 18-24 in (46-60 cm), tail 2-4 in (5-11 cm); weight 3-4 lb (1.5-2 kg); large ears, as long as 5-8 in (12.5-20 cm), with black tips; sandy brown coat with a black tail; a black stripe down to the rump

● **Food**
Grasses and plant matter

● **Breeding**
Breeds several times a year, with 1-8 leverets in a litter, more usually 3-4; the young are well developed at birth and can move around almost immediately

● **Status**
Common

◄ *Black-tailed jack rabbits often live in dry habitats such as grasslands and deserts.*

See also **Hare, Rabbit**

Jaguar

KEY FACTS

● **Name**
Jaguar
(*Panthera onca*)

● **Range**
Central and South
America, from
southern U.S. to
central Patagonia

● **Habitat**
Tropical forests,
swamps, savannah

● **Appearance**
A large, heavily built
cat with short, sturdy
legs; males may grow
up to 8 ft (2.5 m)
from head to tail; the
fur is yellowish- or
reddish-brown with
large rosette-shaped
markings and pale
underparts (although
all-black animals are
common)

● **Food**
Some large mammals,
small rodents, birds,
amphibians, fish

● **Breeding**
2-4 cubs are born
blind, 3 months after
mating; the mother
rears them alone,
suckling them for 6
months; cubs can
mate at 3 years

● **Status**
Endangered

The jaguar is a large, powerful South American cat. It belongs to a group of animals known as the "big cats," along with its cousins the lions, tigers, and leopards, and it is the largest cat found in South America. Along with the Snow leopard of central Asia, the jaguar differs from other big cats in that it "coughs" rather than roars, communicating with grunts, snarls, and growls, as well as mewing cries during the mating season.

Stalking the forests

The jaguar is a carnivore (meat eater) and an efficient hunter. Like most other big cats, it cannot run at high speeds for very long in pursuit of its prey, and uses its

▲ *The jaguar is often confused with the leopard: the jaguar (above) is more solidly built, with a large head, short (but strong) limbs, and huge paws. The leopard also has smaller, boxy spots, while the jaguar has large, rosette-like markings.*

strength and short bursts of speed to catch its victims. It also relies heavily on its stealth and the ability to creep up on unsuspecting animals. It then uses the element of surprise to startle and catch them. For this reason, the jaguar prefers to hunt by night under thick cover. It may inhabit open ground if necessary, but can most often be found padding silently through swampland and dense jungle. Indeed, although it mainly hunts on the ground, the jaguar has sharp claws and powerful limbs and can climb trees well.

The jaguar preys on a wide variety of animals, including some large mammals such as tapirs, monkeys, and deer; small rodents, birds, fish, reptiles; and amphibians such as frogs and turtles. The jaguar spends much time near water and is an excellent swimmer.

Defending their patch

Jaguars are generally solitary animals, preferring to hunt alone rather than in pairs or large groups. They are also very territorial and defend their territories fiercely, marking the boundaries with strong-smelling urine. Some animals have even been known to escort humans out of their territories, following them from a safe distance in the jungle without attacking and then disappearing just as suddenly as they appeared!

The size of a jaguar's territory depends on the availability of food in the area and ranges from 2-200 sq miles (5-500 km^2). Occasionally, jaguars undertake long journeys, traveling as far as 500 miles (800 km) at once. Scientists are not yet sure of the reason for this.

During the mating season (which is in spring in the northern parts of the jaguar's range), mating pairs meet up together. Just over three months later, the female gives birth to a litter of two to four young in a specially hidden den in the vegetation and rocks. The cubs weigh a mere 25-30 oz (700-900 g) each and are blind at birth, although they are able to see at about 13 days old. The father is absent while they are growing up, having left

their mother immediately after mating. The female rears them alone, suckling them for three to four months and taking them on hunting trips once they reach the age of six months. She is very protective of them and can be extremely aggressive toward intruders — even their own father! The cubs stay with her until they are two years old, at which age they leave to become independent.

A rare sight

Jaguars have been widely hunted for sport as well as for their beautiful skins, and much of their habitat has been destroyed by humans. Today, all eight subspecies of jaguar are seriously endangered.

▲ *This jaguar is "fishing" for its dinner: it crouches, still and silent by the edge of the water, then flips the fish out onto the rocks with its forepaw.*

NATURAL HABITAT

Jaguar

Jay

Jays are larger than average perching birds, living in trees and woodlands and often found in gardens. The Blue jay of eastern North America is a friendly bird, but in the past many species of jay have been rather unpopular. Jays have acquired a bad reputation for two main reasons: first, they have been seen attacking the nests of other birds in search of food; and second, they are sometimes quite vicious in their attacks on people who approach their nests, particularly just after the young have hatched. However, both these forms of behavior are a natural part of their lifestyle: other birds' nests are attacked only if there is a shortage of other suitable food, and attacks on people are simply a defensive measure.

Jays are cunning, inquisitive and intelligent birds, but their outstanding characteristic is their noisiness. They can be heard announcing the presence of any intruder in the woods with earsplitting shrieks and have a great number of calls,

▲ *This young Blue jay has its feathers fluffed up to protect it from the cold. Those that breed in northern parts may move south for the winter.*

sometimes imitating the screams of hawks and the songs of other birds. But in the spring they have a sweet, musical song that few people recognize, and in the nesting season they are silent and secretive.

Strong feeder

Jays have powerful, all-purpose bills that are very efficient at handling a range of food. They have a very varied diet, including insects, seeds, nuts, berries, and even small reptiles and amphibians. Blue jays are particularly fond of acorns and beechnuts and often store them in the ground for winter. They use their bills to pluck acorns from twigs, and they may

NATURAL HABITAT

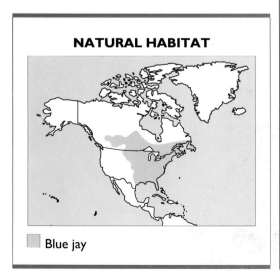

Blue jay

KEY FACTS

● **Name**
Blue jay
(*Cyanocitta cristata*)

● **Range**
Eastern North America from Canada to southern states; those in the northern part of the range move south in flocks in the fall

● **Habitat**
Mixed woodlands, suburban gardens, groves, town parks

● **Appearance**
11-12½ in (28-31 cm); a showy blue bird with a crest; bold white spots on the wings and tail, whitish or dull gray underparts, a black necklace

● **Food**
Omnivorous; mainly vegetable matter

● **Breeding**
Eggs are laid March-July, 3-6, usually 4-5; female incubates eggs for 16½-18 days, young leave the nest when 17-21 days old; adults defend the nest and their young

● **Status**
Common

carry one in the mouth and one in the throat when taking them off to their storehouses. Many of the stored nuts remain uneaten at the end of the winter; when they sprout in the spring they help to replant forests. Most jays and other members of the crow family, including the magpie, like to store food away like this for the leaner winter months. The Gray jay or Canadian jay of northeastern North America has found a slightly different way of storing food. The climate is very cold over its range so, if it were to bury its food for winter, the food would be lost in snow and frozen in the ground. Instead, the Gray jay stores seeds and other food in the foliage of conifers by sticking it to the leaves with saliva.

Careful parents

Although they have a reputation for violence, Blue jays seem to be caring parents. In the spring, pairs work together to build a nest in the angle of a branch of a tree or bush. They usually choose a site about 10-15 ft (3-5 m) above the ground. Both adults break twigs from trees to make a neat framework for the nest, which is about 7-8 in (17-20 cm) in diameter. Blue jays frequently build nests that are never completed or used for breeding. A pair may build several before the breeding nest is started.

They strengthen the outer walls by weaving bark, mosses, and grasses into the twigs and by daubing them with mud. The inside of the cup is lined with fine rootlets. The female takes charge of the eggs until they hatch, but the male helps to guard the nest and flies at any intruders, dive-bombing and pecking them. Besides attacking humans, Blue jays sometimes mob birds of prey such as hawks or owls. The first bird to see the predator calls to attract other jays. The jays perch around the predator, calling loudly and diving down at it, but rarely actually touching it. This may continue for half an hour or so, until the predator moves away or the jays give up.

Relatives around the world

The Common or European jay (*Garrulus glandarius*) is a similar size to the Blue jay, with a similar lifestyle but predominantly pink coloring. It is found all over Europe and in many parts of Asia, right across to Japan. Much more colorful, however, are the jays of Central and South America and those of Southeast Asia. These forest-dwelling birds are a little larger than the jays of more temperate countries.

▼ *This Steller's jay (Cyanocitta stelleri) is closely related to the Blue jay, but is found in the western part of North America. Its head is darker in color, and its underparts are blue rather than white. Jays have strong bills and defend their nests fiercely, but they may become quite tame if you feed them regularly. However, they tend to bully other birds, so it is a good idea to set up a separate bird feeder if you want to attract jays to your garden.*

Jellyfish

Jellyfish can be found in every ocean of the world, from the warm tropical seas to the icy polar regions. Most species live near the surface and have bowl-shaped bodies that measure from under an inch to a foot (2-30 cm) in diameter. Beneath their bodies hang long arms and tentacles. Although their bodies are usually colorless, their internal organs can be any color from orange to violet.

Here's the sting

Despite their defenseless and delicate appearance, most of the 250 species of jellyfish are active predators and they can catch and kill large prey such as fish. Even those species that feed on animals so small they can only be seen under a microscope have hidden weapons and are able to protect themselves against the largest predators in the sea. Their dangling tentacles carry poisons to stun their prey. The poison used by some species of jellyfish is very dangerous even to

▲ The Portuguese man-of-war is a large, deadly, poisonous jellyfish that has tentacles as long as 45 ft (15 m) hanging below its floating body.

humans. The Australian Sea Wasp, *Chironex fleckeri,* can cause death in humans within minutes. The sting of a Portuguese man-of-war may cause nausea and shock as well as a burning feeling or numbness.

Because jellyfish do not appear to move much they are often thought of as being inactive, but if the tentacles and arms that hang lazily from the body are magnified, the true nature of the jellyfish is revealed.

NATURAL HABITAT

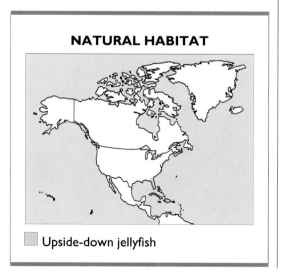

Upside-down jellyfish

In some species the tentacles are short and form a frill around the edge of their bodies. These tentacles beat rapidly, forcing water and tiny animals toward the jellyfish's sticky arms. Once the food has stuck to them, it is carried to the mouth and scraped off.

Not all jellyfish feed this way. The North Atlantic giant violet jellyfish (*Cyanea capillata*), which can grow up to 6 ft 9 in (2 m) in diameter, also has extremely long tentacles – up to 117 ft (33.7 m) long. These tentacles spread out like a vast spider's web beneath it. Any small animals that brush against them are instantly harpooned by hundreds of barbed and poisonous darts. At the same time, the tentacle coils up to bring the food up to the mouth where it is swallowed.

Versatile feeders

Another way of gathering food can be seen in the Upside-down jellyfish. These jellyfish have given up floating and have settled on the seabed in the shallow waters around Florida and the West Indies. Here they have flipped themselves upside down so that their frilly arms can move freely in the water. They feed in the same way as the Common jellyfish, picking tiny particles out of the water. However, they can also get energy from sunlight: algae in their arms convert it into food the same way as plants do.

Multiplying numbers

Jellyfish have a complicated life cycle compared to most animals. Adult jellyfish are either male or female and produce either sperm or eggs. The sperm float in the water until taken in by the female. Jellyfish often gather together in vast numbers at certain times of the year to increase the chance of fertilization. Once the sperm has fertilized the eggs, the female releases them into the water and leaves them to float away. In the Common jellyfish they stick to one of its arms and remain there until they hatch.

The larva looks completely different from the adult. It is flat with small tentacles around the edge of its body that it uses like little oars, pushing itself through the water. After a few days of swimming freely the larva starts to sink. As it touches the seabed, a stalk begins to grow from underneath the larva's body. This will soon attach it firmly to the sea bed. After a while, the short tentacles that were used for swimming grow longer and are soon capable of catching food.

As the larva gets bigger it splits its top half from its bottom half. The bottom half then continues to split in half. After about a week there is a stack of developing jellyfish. Once these young jellyfish are self-sufficient, they break off from the stack and float off to grow into adults.

KEY FACTS

● **Name**
Upside-down jellyfish (*Cassiopeia* species)

● **Range**
Florida and the West Indies

● **Habitat**
Shallow seas around coasts, mangroves

● **Appearance**
Up to 12 in (29 cm) in diameter; cauliflower-like arms

● **Food**
Microscopic plants and animals; energy from algae

● **Breeding**
Eggs hatch into larvae; the larvae split into many jellyfish; no parental care

● **Status**
Widespread, but pollution could soon be a problem

◀ *The bluish arms of the Upside-down jellyfish contain small, plant-like organisms that can supply all the food the jellyfish needs. The algae take energy from sunlight by a process called photosynthesis.*

Kangaroo

Everyone knows that kangaroos, members of the marsupial group of mammals, live in Australia. What many do not know is that kangaroos, and the closely related wallabies, come in all shapes and sizes. The tree kangaroos look like large squirrels with long tails, small ears, and squirrel-like faces. Another group of less well-known kangaroos are the rat kangaroos in the *Potaridae* family. Living up to their name, the nine species in this family look very much like rats and mice.

A typical roo

Of the 45 species of kangaroo, the best known is the Red kangaroo, one of 37 species of large-footed kangaroos whose family name, *Macropodidae*, is extremely descriptive (in Greek, *macro* means large and *pod* means foot). The Red kangaroo has large, flat feet, strong legs, and a long muscular tail to balance itself as it hops

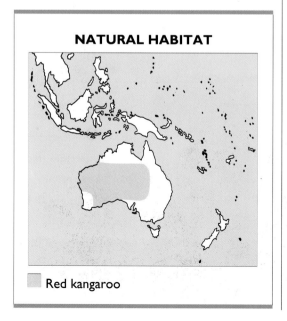

NATURAL HABITAT

Red kangaroo

along. The front legs are small and used while feeding but not while the animal hops at high speed, and the arms are relatively short. They are mainly nocturnal animals, with large ears to help them hear better at night.

Along with the big feet and tail, the Red kangaroo is best known for its pouch. Most mammals the size of the Red kangaroo have a pregnancy that lasts around 6 months. Red kangaroos have extremely short gestation times — the young develop in the womb for only 33 days. When a baby kangaroo is born it is

▲ *Male kangaroos "box" with each other to gain access to females, balancing themselves with their muscular tails. The Red kangaroo (shown above) is the largest of all the kangaroos, weighing up to 200 lb (90 kg) – so don't volunteer to enter a boxing contest with one!*

tiny, blind, hairless, and only about an inch (2.5 cm) long. The only parts of the body that are well developed are the arms, which the baby uses to crawl up the mother's belly into the pouch. The mother does not help the young get to the pouch in any way.

Once in the pouch, the baby attaches itself to one of the mother's teats and spends almost 9 months growing in the pouch. In a way, this "pouch time" is like a second gestation. While in the pouch, the baby kangaroo is known as a joey.

Extra numbers

Life is not easy for a Red kangaroo. Extreme variation in rainfall means that young in the pouch, or even year-old animals that live out of the pouch, often starve to death. However, because of her reproductive system, the Red kangaroo always has another baby ready to replace any that are lost. At any time, a female may have three young at different stages of development: a joey in the pouch, an older yearling outside the pouch, and a fertilized egg waiting for the pouch to become free.

As soon as a baby is born and crawls into the pouch, the female mates and an egg is fertilized. But instead of developing normally, the egg stops growing and waits in the mother's womb. If the joey dies or leaves the pouch, the egg begins developing and about a month later another baby is born.

▼ *Kangaroos are well known for the way they hop across the grasslands. This mother probably has a second baby in her pouch. While the baby feeds on a rich, creamy milk, a second teat provides watery food for the older offspring.*

Kangaroo rat

KEY FACTS

● **Name**
Merriam's
kangaroo rat
(*Dipodomys merriami*)

● **Range**
Southwestern North
America

● **Habitat**
Deserts

● **Appearance**
Head and body
length of 6 in
(16 cm); pale brown
upperparts and white
beneath with a white
stripe running over
the back; a large
head and large eyes;
short forepaws; long
hind legs; a long tail
measuring 5-6 in
(13-16 cm), ending in
a tuft of fur; some
individuals may weigh
up to 5 oz (150 g)

● **Food**
Seeds, leaves, fruit,
plant stems

● **Breeding**
Females bear up to
3 litters of 1-3 young
per year, usually
about 4 weeks after
mating; the young
remain in the burrow
for 6 weeks

● **Status**
Widespread

The kangaroo rat (not to be confused with the rat kangaroo) is a small creature with long hind legs and tail and a habit of hopping erratically from place to place. It is because the kangaroo rat shares these features with the kangaroo of Australia that it was given its common name. Similar features are also found in the jerboa and the kangaroo mouse, which, like the kangaroo rat, inhabit dry places.

Kangaroo rats are rodents and belong to the same family as pocket mice and kangaroo mice. There are some 24 species of kangaroo rat, all of which are found in western and southern North America.

The kangaroo rat lives in dry or semidry regions. It favors open country with little vegetation where it can move about easily, and sandy soil that is easy to dig. During

▲ *Like this Merriam's kangaroo rat, most species have coloring that is pale brown above and white underneath. Some may have a white stripe on each hip and a furry tuft at the end of their tails.*

the day it hides in its burrow beneath the ground and does not emerge until it is completely dark. Unlike many other animals that are active at night, the kangaroo rat shuns all kind of light, remaining in its burrow even when there is bright moonlight. It will also stay beneath ground if it is very wet.

Surviving the heat
The kangaroo rat is well adapted to its hot dry habitat. It can survive for long periods without drinking because its body processes are able to extract water from

food, especially from succulent plants. However, it does obtain some water from drinking dew. By resting up during the day, the kangaroo rat avoids high temperatures. If it does get overheated, it can lower its body temperature by producing large amounts of saliva and licking its entire body. As the saliva evaporates in the heat, the body cools down. The kangaroo rat also takes frequent dust baths. These free the fur of foreign particles, which prevents it from getting matted and stops sores from developing on the skin.

Processing their food

Kangaroo rats feed on a wide variety of plants and eat almost every part – seeds, stems, leaves, and fruit. They will also eat insects occasionally. They hoard away some of the food they find in food stores placed near their nests, ready to use when food and water is scarce.

The kangaroo rat transports its food to the store in special cheek pouches. These are made of folds of skin and are lined with fur. To remove the food in its pouches, the kangaroo rat places its forepaws on its cheeks and squeezes until the food spills out.

Scientists have found evidence that the kangaroo rats process at least some of their food before storing it. They place it in shallow hollows in the sand and leave it there until it has dried out. This helps to preserve the food so that it doesn't get moldy. Then they transport it to more permanent food stores.

Owls and rattlesnakes prey on the kangaroo rat. Its main defense against

these predators is its highly developed hearing. Scientists have shown that kangaroo rats can pick up the faintest rustling sounds from a considerable distance, even the soft swish of a bird's wings or the movement of a snake's body over the earth.

A good listener

Such sensitive hearing is made possible by a special mechanism in which dome-shaped bones lie over the middle ears, making noises sound louder. Devices such as these are very important to animals living in deserts, where it is vital to be able to detect predators from a distance. In addition, it is thought that these special organs may help the kangaroo rat to balance while sitting up and leaping about.

▲ *Kangaroo rats, like this Ord kangaroo rat from Arizona, generally forage for food under cover of shrubs. This means that they are less vulnerable to attack from predators.*

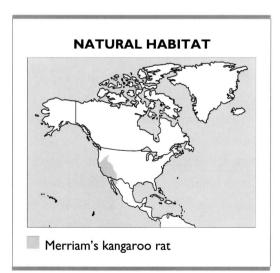

NATURAL HABITAT

Merriam's kangaroo rat

Kestrel

Kestrels are among the most highly specialized birds of prey. Their long narrow wings are made for lengthy, swift flight. Strong beaks and equally strong feet with sharp talons are ideally suited to a hunting lifestyle and also play a part in defense, particularly among the young.

Kestrels are the smallest and the most common birds belonging to the falcon group. They are found on all of the world's continents with the exception of Antarctica. In North America the species

▲ *Sometimes, instead of hovering in midair, the kestrel will hunt from a convenient post. Unlike other falcons, it rarely catches prey on the wing, but it has been seen to steal another bird's catch while in flight.*

are represented by the American kestrel, which is also popularly known as the Sparrow hawk (not to be confused with the European sparrowhawk *Accipiter nisus*, which is a separate species). In Europe and Africa the main species is the Common kestrel. Both the Common and the American kestrels are very similar in habits and appearance.

Country or city dweller?

The kestrel usually inhabits open or fairly open countryside, often near woodlands. However, in some places it also takes up residence in cities, where it has shown a remarkable ability to adapt to the urban environment. It is perhaps best known for its habit of hovering, and for this reason is sometimes known as the windhover.

The kestrel hovers in midair up to 100 ft (about 30 m) above the ground, using its remarkably keen eyesight to watch for the movements of small creatures on the earth below. It hunts over open spaces

NATURAL HABITAT

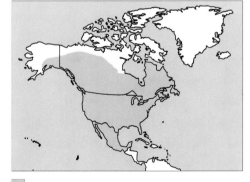

☐ American kestrel

- **Name**
American kestrel or Sparrow hawk (*Falco sparverius*)

- **Range**
Most of North and South America except the tundra; birds in Canada and mountainous areas may migrate south for the winter

- **Habitat**
Open countryside, cities

- **Appearance**
9-11 in (23-28 cm) from head to tail; adults have rusty backs barred with black and rusty tails with black bars at the tip; dark blue inner wings; the head has patches of white, black, and rust

- **Food**
Rodents, small birds, insects; occasionally carrion, meat, and bread scraps from bird feeders

- **Breeding**
4-6 eggs, buff-brown thickly speckled with dark reddish-brown; the eggs hatch after 4 weeks and the young birds fledge 4 weeks after that

- **Status**
Widespread

such as unused land, the side of the highway, a field, or a grassy plain. In such places it may hover for an hour, fixing its eyes on the ground and watching for any movement indicating the presence of a small creature. Every now and again the bird will drop to the ground to capture its prey. The main items in the kestrel's diet are small mammals such as rodents, small birds, earthworms, and large insects such as grasshoppers and moths.

Acrobatic displays

Kestrels normally begin their courtship in the spring – usually late March or early April. They do not build nests themselves; instead they often take over the abandoned nests of other fairly large birds such as crows, buzzards, and magpies. Kestrels also nest in hollow trees, on cliff ledges and, in cities, in crevices and on ledges on tall buildings.

▲ *This kestrel has spotted its prey (probably a small rodent) in the grass and has dropped to the ground to seize it in its long, sharp talons.*

The courtship display of the male kestrel consists of a series of aerial acrobatics with which he tries to attract the attention of the female and draw her to the nesting site. He flies around in circles above the perched female, taking three or four wing beats and following these with a glide. This flight is interspersed with dives. Throughout the display he utters the characteristic cry "kee-kee-kee." Sometimes the female will fly up from her perch to join him, while the male continues flying around and above her.

Four to six eggs are laid and are kept warm – usually by the female, although sometimes by the male, who also feeds the female. The chicks hatch in about four weeks and grow feathers four weeks later.

Killdeer

▲ *From western North America, down to Argentina, the killdeer is a common sight near lakes, rivers, and shores. Its long legs enable it to wade through shallow waters in search of food, but it is also at home in drier grassland habitats.*

Throughout North America, in those areas that are not covered in snow, and as far south as Peru and Chile, the plaintive "killdee, killdee" of the killdeer can be heard along seashore, lakes, and rivers. Of course it is this call that gives the killdeer its name; and it is such a sad, distressing sound that many people, when they hear it for the first time, think that it must be the cry of a young bird or a bird in pain.

The killdeer is probably the most widely distributed and best known of all North American wading birds. However, although it is well adapted for life along the water's edge, the killdeer (unlike most shorebirds) is often found many miles from water, in open fields and grasslands.

Family likeness

The killdeer is a type of plover. It is a small, noisy bird, with a neat, tapering body and pert, round head. Its most distinctive marking, if you are trying to distinguish between several similar grassland and marshland birds, is a double ring of black feathers across the upper part of its breast — one of these bands extends right around the killdeer's neck.

When on the ground it moves like other plovers, running in short bursts at quite a speed. It struts around the grassland, probing the ground with its strong, straight bill, looking for insects and grubs. It can also be seen along shorelines and riverbanks, dipping its bill into the muddy banks in search of aquatic insects. It often follows plows in its hunt for a tasty meal, searching for worms and larvae that have been exposed. When it takes to the air its flight is swift but erratic; it flies low and skims the ground.

Breeding patterns

Spring is the mating season, and killdeers perform a ritual mating display. They hover high above the ground and circle over a suitable nesting site. The nest is simply a shallow dip in the ground lined with fine twigs and grasses.

Killdeers are caring parents who protect their eggs and young by flying into the

▲ *The killdeer lays its eggs in a hollow in the ground. The parents are surprisingly well-camouflaged against the rocky scrublands. Even if the parents leave the nest for a short time, the eggs are relatively safe because they, too, are well camouflaged by their buff color with dark spots.*

faces of intruding animals or people. They are also skilled actors who perform what is referred to as the "broken wing act." This involves pretending that one of their wings is broken and running away from the nest, calling piteously and dragging one wing and their tail along the ground. This draws predators away from the nesting site, protecting the young birds.

For the first 10 days after hatching, however, the young killdeers are open to attack and many die before reaching adulthood. It is about three weeks before they are able to fly.

Killdeers are seldom seen in large flocks: they tend to forage on their own, or in pairs during the breeding season. Occasionally, however, groups of up to 50 have been seen patrolling the grasslands and making their characteristic short flights. They are extremely noisy birds, which gives them their Latin name, *Charadrius vociferus.*

NATURAL HABITAT

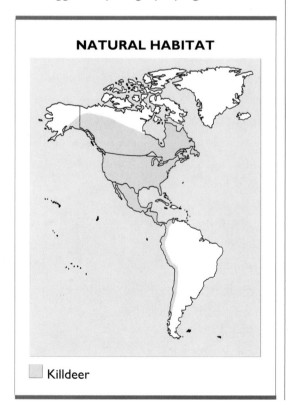

Killdeer

Killer whale

The Killer whale, or orca, is a large, striking looking dolphin. Along with other dolphins, it belongs to the group of toothed whales. Many people believe, because of its common name, that the Killer whale must be a maneater. It is a ferocious killer, but has never been known to attack or kill humans; rather it gets its name from the fact that it preys on other dolphins and whales, as well as seals, sea lions, sea birds, squid, and fish.

Largest and fastest

The Killer whale is one of the most distinctive members of the dolphin group. It is the largest dolphin, with males growing up to 33 ft (10 m) long and weighing as much as 9 tons (8100 kg). It is colored black and white, with an unmistakable white spot above and behind the eye. Unlike other dolphins, its large flippers are rounded like paddles, and it has a tall, triangular fin on its back that may stand as high as $6\frac{1}{2}$ ft (2 m). It also has a large, rounded head, without the characteristic dolphin "beak" shape.

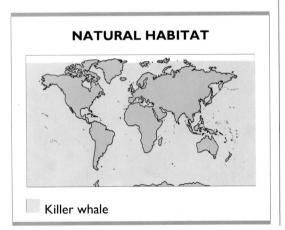

NATURAL HABITAT

Killer whale

One of the most fascinating things about Killer whales is their hunting technique. They live in large groups called pods, which hunt for food together, cooperating in a way that is unusual for most sea mammals. Most of the animals in each pod are related, and there is a strong social bond holding them together, usually for life. The pods are generally made up of one male, several females, and their young, although there may be up to 40 animals. The pod's range may be between 200 and 300 sq miles (320 and 480 km^2).

Killer whales are extremely efficient predators. Unlike other dolphins and whales, they prey on warm-blooded animals as well as squid and fish. They tend to target smaller creatures such as seals, turtles, and other dolphins, but they have even been known to harass and kill large whales much bigger than themselves, such as the Blue whale!

▲ *When they want to look out for any prey or find out what is going on around them, Killer whales may poke their heads into the air while resting vertically in the water. This is sometimes known as "spy-hopping."*

See also **Dolphin**

KEY FACTS

● **Name**
Killer whale
(*Orcinus orca*)

● **Range**
All oceans; especially the colder Arctic and Antarctic waters

● **Habitat**
Occasionally open seas, but more often coastal waters

● **Appearance**
A large dolphin, measuring up to 33 ft (10 m) in males, females smaller, up to 28 ft (8.5 m); black back and sides, white underparts, a white mark above and behind the eye, and a white patch extending onto the flank; large, paddle-like flippers and a tall fin measuring up to 6½ ft (2 m), with a gray "saddle" behind

● **Food**
Other dolphins and whales, seals, sea lions, sea birds, turtles, squid, fish

● **Breeding**
A single calf is born, measuring about 8 ft (2.5 m) at birth; the calf suckles for at least 1 year

● **Status**
Common in much of its range

Spying for food

The members of a Killer whale pod communicate with a series of underwater sounds — each pod has its own "dialect" made up of clicks, whistles, and pulses. When they detect a school of fish, the dolphins swim toward them in a long line, herding them until they have them trapped between themselves and the shoreline. Then individuals swim forward, picking off the fish one by one until they are no longer hungry.

Killer whales also have a spectacular way of catching seal or sea lion pups. Sometimes they break through thick sheets of ice from below in order to catch animals resting on top; other times they purposely run aground on the shore as the waves crash up the beach, grabbing an unsuspecting pup in their huge jaws. This intentional stranding has the effect of panicking the animals into jumping into the water to escape, straight into the jaws of other members of the pod.

As the Killer whale is carried back into the sea on the waves, it kills its catch by throwing it into the air and thrashing it through the water, often slapping it with its powerful tail. Although the Killer whale has about 20 large, strong teeth in its jaws, it is not able to chew its food and swallows it whole or rips off chunks.

A big baby

Female Killer whales give birth to one calf at a time, in some cases only once every eight years. The calf is born about 15 months after mating and is very well developed at birth, already measuring up to 8 ft (2.5 m).

The calf is weaned after a year, although it may stay with its mother until it is about three years old. Then male Killer whales usually leave to find and join another pod, while females remain for life in the pod in which they were born. Scientists have estimated that the Killer whale's natural lifespan is between 50 and 100 years.

▼ *The Killer whale is the fastest dolphin in the world and can swim at up to 30 mph (45 km/h).*

Kingfisher

Many of us think of kingfishers as small, brightly colored birds that are seen at the edges of ponds or rivers, darting into the shallow water to catch fish, their favorite food. However, the Kingfisher family contains 95 different species of birds that are found throughout the world in a variety of habitats and feed on a wide range of food.

The Kingfisher family is split into two subfamilies: the forest kingfishers (*Daceloninae*) and the fish-eating kingfishers (*Alcedininae*). Only three species are found in North America: the Green kingfisher and the Ringed kingfisher, which are South and Central American species that can be found in some southern states, and the Belted kingfisher, which is found throughout North America.

King of the fishers

The fish-eating kingfishers are fairly small, squat birds with large heads and short tails. They have long, sharp-pointed beaks, sometimes colored red or yellow, which are extremely strong and well adapted to catching fish. Many of them, such as the Common kingfisher of Eurasia and northern Africa, have bright, distinctive feathers (often greens and blues), and some have large, upward-standing crests on top of their heads. Their legs, which are only used for perching, are very short, and they have unusual feet with three toes pointing forward and one backward. They can fly fast and straight, but not very far.

These birds are skilled fishers. They have regular perches – usually a branch overhanging a river or pond, or a stake on a pier along the coast – where they sit, upright and motionless, watching for their prey. Once they have spotted a fish, they dive headlong into the water, seizing it in their tough beaks. They have to aim well as they do this, because they close their eyes under water.

Some species do not use a perch, but hover above the water until they spot their prey. These kingfishers will also catch and eat large tadpoles, crabs,

▲ *This brightly colored Common kingfisher (Alcedo atthis) is flying back to its nest in a riverbank, with a fish gripped tightly in its beak.*

KEY FACTS

● **Name**
Belted kingfisher (*Ceryle alcyon*)

● **Range**
Alaska and Canada, down to southern U.S.; winters in northern South America and the Galapagos Islands

● **Habitat**
Usually near water; streams, lakes, bays, coasts

● **Appearance**
Medium-sized bird, measuring 13 in (33 cm) from head to tail, with a large head and bill; blue-gray above and white below with a bushy crest and a broad gray breast band; females also have a rusty breastband

● **Food**
Mainly fish; also large tadpoles, insects, crustaceans, young birds, small mammals

● **Breeding**
5-8 white eggs are laid from April to July and are incubated for 23-24 days

● **Status**
Widespread

374

▲ **When it has caught a fish, the kingfisher flies back to its perch, where it beats the fish against the wood to kill it. Then the bird swallows it whole, tossing it in the air so that it is swallowed headfirst. Any food that the kingfisher cannot digest is brought up again in small pellets. This picture is of a male Belted kingfisher (Ceryle alcyon) – the female is similar but has a band of rust-colored feathers across her chest.**

crayfish, insects, young birds, and even small mammals. As well as looking out for food, the kingfisher must be aware of any predators in the area, such as falcons or hawks. If they are attacked by these large birds of prey, they will often dive below the surface of the water to escape.

The forest kingfishers are perhaps less familiar to most people than their cousins. They are generally larger in size than the fish-eating species and their bills are often wider and flatter. Many of them live far from water, in dry savannahs or forests, and they feed on large insects and small reptiles, birds, amphibians, and mammals. The largest species is the Australian Kookaburra or Laughing Jackass, so called because of its strange "laughing" cries that can be heard at dawn and dusk.

Kingfishers are solitary birds, spending their time alone in small feeding territories except during the breeding season in the spring and summer. Then males and females meet together to defend larger territories that contain their nesting and feeding areas.

Nesting in the riverbanks

The fishing species dig their burrows in riverbanks, using their bills to dig and pushing out the dirt with their feet. These are usually tunnels 3-7 ft (1-2 m) long, extending horizontally and ending in a large, unlined chamber. The forest kingfishers also nest in holes, although some species such as the Kookaburra prefer hollow trees, and some tropical species use abandoned termite nests.

Many species of kingfisher have two broods of young per year, but the Belted kingfisher only lays one clutch of six or seven white eggs. These are incubated by both parents for 23-24 days. The young are naked, blind, and totally defenseless when they hatch. They stay in the nest for three or four weeks, during which time they are fed on fish and crustaceans by the male and female.

NATURAL HABITAT

Belted kingfisher

See also **Kookaburra**

Kite

▲ *This Brahminy kite is swooping down to the water to catch a fish with its large, powerful feet.*

Kites are lightly built birds with small heads, long, narrow wings, and long tails. They are birds of prey and are closely related to eagles and vultures. They fly fairly fast, flapping and then gliding with their wings angled back, but they do not fly fast enough to catch small birds in flight. Most kites eat some dead prey (carrion), and they will also take prey from ospreys and falcons, mobbing them until they drop their victims.

Kites make up three groups or subfamilies: the true kites, the white-tailed kites, and the fork-tailed kites. The true kites are represented in North America by the Snail kite and the Mississippi kite. Two other species of kite are found in North America – the Swallow-tailed kite and the White-tailed kite.

Snail kites

Throughout its range, the Snail kite lives in swamps or marshes where a particular kind of freshwater snail occurs. This snail is almost the only source of food for the Snail kite. The snail remains under water for much of the day, but comes to the surface to feed on marsh vegetation in the early morning and later afternoon.

The bird's hunting strategy is to fly slowly over open channels and pools, now and then hovering awkwardly like a gull. When it spots a snail, the kite plunges toward the water and seizes the creature with its feet. It then takes the food to a perch, where it uses its hooked beak to

KEY FACTS

● **Name**
Snail or Everglade kite (*Rostrhamus sociabilis*)

● **Range**
Florida, Cuba, and from eastern Mexico south to Argentina and Uruguay

● **Habitat**
Marshland

● **Appearance**
Male is black with grayish tones over the underparts; white on the base and tip of the tail and wing coverts; the female is sooty brown above with mottled underparts; the flight feathers are barred light brown; the length from head to tail is 15 in (38 cm)

● **Food**
Mainly freshwater snails, but will also eat meat in captivity

● **Breeding**
Both parents incubate the 2- 4 eggs; the young leave the nest 30 days after the eggs are laid

● **Status**
Rare in Florida and Cuba

extract the snail from its shell. As the Snail kite is largely dependent on this one type of food, it cannot survive where its habitat has been destroyed. Measures taken to drain large areas of the Florida Everglades for farming are largely responsible for the bird's rarity in this part of its northern range.

Like other hawks, the male Snail kite displays in the air during courtship, soaring up to 100 ft (30 m) above the ground and then plunging toward the earth with wings folded back. Sometimes it somersaults head over tail. Both male and female birds build the nest just above the water surface in a low bush or in tall grasses. It is usually made up of grass and weeds put together untidily.

The White-tailed kite is a medium-sized hawk found in the southwestern United States and southern South America, where it lives in parks, wooded grasslands, river valleys, and foothills. It preys on large insects, rodents, and lizards. After declining in number, this bird is now becoming reestablished in California and Texas.

The Swallow-tailed kite is a graceful bird about 24 in (60 cm) long. The plumage over its back is black with a metallic sheen; the head, neck and breast are white. When it is at rest, its wings cross each other at the tips. Its long tail is forked, emphasizing the bird's resemblance to the swallow, especially when flying.

Flying in large groups

The Swallow-tailed kite associates with other birds of the same species and can sometimes be seen flying in groups of 40-50 individuals. During the breeding season, several of these kites will make their nests close to each other.

The Swallow-tailed kite's diet consists mainly of large insects and tree frogs, but it also eats eggs, small birds, reptiles, and even fruit. Using its feet, it catches food while it is in flight. This bird also drinks on the wing, flying low over the water in the same way as a swallow.

NATURAL HABITAT

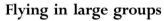
Snail kite

▲ *This Snail kite is surveying its territory from its vantage point high above the treetops. This species is now very rare in the United States and is much more common throughout parts of Central and South America east of the Andes. In North America it is found only in the Florida Everglades.*

See also **Falcon, Hawk, Osprey**

Kiwi

The kiwi is famous as the national bird of New Zealand. It is a flightless bird, because on the islands where it lives there were no large mammals to attack it and it simply did not need to use its wings. Kiwis are shy, retiring birds, so it is unusual to see them in the wild. They are becoming rarer as humans and mammals invade their territory. There are three species, all very similar, living in different parts of New Zealand.

Feathered shape

While most birds have different types of feathers on different parts of their body (long tail and wing feathers and shorter feathers on the head and breast), kiwis are covered with feathers of an even length and similar texture. They look like round, brown furry mammals with long noses, more like anteaters than birds. The feathers are predominantly dark brown, but in some species they are streaked and mottled with a paler shade.

They do have wings, which are about 2 in (5 cm) long, but they can hardly move them. There are bare patches beneath the wings, and when it sleeps, the kiwi tucks its head under its wing. Their legs are stout and strong, and spaced quite

KEY FACTS

● **Name**
Common or Brown kiwi (*Apteryx australis*)

● **Range**
South Island and Stewart Island, New Zealand

● **Habitat**
Forests

● **Appearance**
20 in (50 cm); a round, brown bird with a long beak; stout gray legs

● **Food**
Carnivorous; mainly worms, insects, centipedes

● **Breeding**
One or two large white eggs laid in a burrow dug by the male; incubated by the male

● **Status**
Widespread within a limited range

◄ *Looking more like a hairy mammal with lizard-like feet than a feathered bird, the Brown kiwi is well disguised in the forests of New Zealand.*

widely apart, so that as it walks or runs it rolls from side to side.

Foraging for food

The kiwi has a much keener sense of smell than most other birds: its nostrils are at the tip of its beak so it can sniff out the grubs and worms that are its favorite food. The kiwi only comes out to forage at night – another reason why so few are seen in the wild.

The whole time they forage, pairs of kiwis call to each other with a distinctive, loud, sometimes rasping call so that they can stay together and keep control of their territory. The breeding season is long: eggs may be laid anytime from late winter to late summer. The male takes a couple of months to prepare the nest – a burrow in the ground. The female lays a single egg or occasionally two. Like most other flightless birds, the male usually takes charge of the incubation of the egg, which is large (as much as a quarter of the weight of the female). The eggs have very

rich, large yolks, and the incubation period is very long – the eggs do not hatch until about 12 weeks after they have been laid. By this time, the young birds have already developed their feathers inside the egg. The food provided by the yolk keeps them going until they are old enough to forage for themselves.

The introduction of predatory mammals such as stoats, weasels, cats, and dogs has drastically reduced the number of kiwis. Also in some places their habitat is being restricted by modern development. Teams of people try to catch and move the kiwis before their habitat is destroyed, and many have been moved to New Zealand's animal reserves. One species, the Little spotted kiwi, became extinct in its original range, but before it died out, it was captured and later released to roam wild on a small island, where it has thrived.

▲ *Because they cannot fly, and because there are few predators to attack their young, kiwis build their nests at ground level. This kiwi is looking after its young in a burrow beneath a log. The young kiwis already have their feathers when they hatch and are soon able to go out to hunt for food themselves.*

NATURAL HABITAT

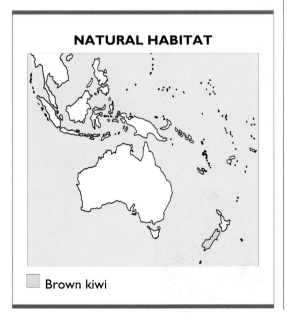

☐ Brown kiwi

Koala

Koalas, sometimes called koala bears, are not even distantly related to the bear family. Like every native mammal of Australia, the koala is a marsupial, or pouched mammal, and newborn koalas spend the first weeks of their lives in the pouch. Physically, koalas are also very different from bears. They are much smaller – they only weigh 15-18 lb (7-9 kg) – and have small bodies and relatively large arms.

Special food

Some animals are not choosy about what they eat: the African elephant eats almost any plant material; and the Red fox eats anything it can find, even taking food from garbage cans. Scientists call those animals generalists. Other animals, called diet specialists, will only eat certain foods. These animals include species such as the Giant panda, which eats only bamboo, and the koala, whose taste for leaves extends only to eucalyptus trees.

Specialist feeders frequently eat things that other animals do not like or cannot digest. The panda's bamboo diet is very rough and difficult to eat, leaving most of the bamboo for the pandas who like the challenge! For most animals, the strong flavor and bitterness of eucalyptus prevents them from eating the leaves of these trees. You might have come across the penetrating scent and flavor of eucalyptus in cold remedies and cough drops. The koala, however, has developed a taste for these leaves and is able to specialize in eucalyptus.

The koala is adapted to eating eucalyptus in several different ways. To begin with, it releases a special chemical from its liver, which helps digest the leaves. In addition, it has special bacteria in its digestive system that break down the chemicals found in eucalyptus leaves. A diet of leaves, and nothing but leaves, is also very hard on the teeth; leaves are full of a chemical called silica, the same substance that sand is made from. To avoid wearing out its teeth, the koala has broad, flat, hardwearing back teeth, or molars, that easily crush and process the leaves it eats.

▲ *The young koala, once it has emerged from the pouch, spends much time on its mother's back. She forages for tender eucalyptus shoots.*

KEY FACTS

- **Name**
Koala (*Phascolarctos cinereus*)

- **Range**
Southeastern Australia

- **Habitat**
Eucalyptus forests below an altitude of 2000 ft (600 m)

- **Appearance**
Gray to reddish-gray coat, white belly and ear fringes; large black claws and a large rectangular nose; adults weigh 11-18 lb (5-8 kg), with males being about 20 percent larger than females

- **Food**
Very specific in its diet, eats only the leaves of trees in the Genus *Eucalyptus*

- **Breeding**
A single young weighing 1 lb (0.5 kg) is born after a gestation of 35 days; the young spends many months in the pouch and is only weaned at 5 months

- **Status**
Common within a small range

Family life

Most koalas live alone, although occasionally they form small groups of two females and their young. Both males and females hold territories, with the male having a larger territory that covers the territories of several females and, perhaps, one or more nonbreeding males. Breeding takes place in the spring (November in the southern hemisphere). Males mate with several females, but females usually mate with only a single male. After a short gestation (pregnancy) of 35 days, a small baby is born, weighing a pound or so (0.5 kg). Like its relatives, kangaroos, the baby then spends several months in the mother's pouch, where it is safe and near its food supply – mother's milk.

Perhaps the greatest misunderstanding over koalas concerns their behavior. Although they are small and fluffy, they can hardly be described as sweet and cuddly. Koalas, in fact, have a reputation for being unsociable and rather nasty, using their sharp claws not only to climb

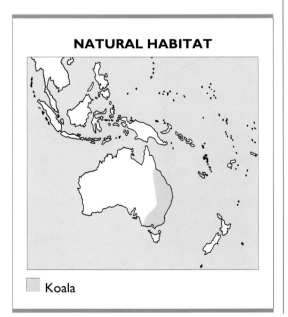

NATURAL HABITAT

Koala

trees, but also to fend off predators and fight off intruders in the breeding season. They are slow-moving creatures, eating and sleeping most of the time.

Koalas are common where there is the right food and environment. Obviously, their great dependence on eucalyptus forests means that they can only exist in areas with this particular type of tree. In some national parks, koalas have become so numerous that many young do not survive because there is not enough food.

To protect these populations, and to expand the area available to koalas, the Australian government has begun a program to move koalas to colonize new eucalyptus forests; they have also been moved to offshore islands where eucalyptus exists, but where koalas never lived because they could not cross the sea.

In the United States, koalas have been introduced to San Diego, on the west coast. Eucalyptus trees brought from Australia provide a habitat for them.

▲ *When the koala leaps from tree to tree, it can grab hold of branches with its clawed paws. Its "thumb" and "forefinger" wrap around one way, while the remaining three fingers wrap around the branch the other way to give a firm grip.*

Komodo dragon

► *It is difficult to see how a lizard as large as the Komodo dragon could hide, but it suddenly leaps out of hiding to attack its prey. Adults work together to tear apart carcasses of dead animals such as this goat. Goats were introduced to the islands where the dragons live, and their habit of attacking such domesticated animals made them unpopular with local people. They are now endangered.*

The Komodo dragon is the largest living lizard. It can grow to over 10 ft (3 m) in length and is not only larger, but also bulkier than most lizards. Usually, a lizard's tail represents about two thirds of its length, but with these monsters, the tail is only half its total length. Komodo dragons prowl around the islands where they live on stout legs with long claws, looking like a dinosaur or monster from a science fiction movie.

Komodo dragons are not the only lizards to be compared with dinosaurs. When scientists first discovered fossils of dinosaurs, they thought that they were the fossils of some long-extinct members of the lizard family. They called them dinosaurs, combining two Greek words, meaning fearful lizard. The lizard suborder as a whole is known as *Sauria*.

Great lengths

These giants among lizards are only found on a few islands in the island chain of Indonesia east of Java. They were first found on the island of Komodo at the beginning of the twentieth century. Here there were no big cats or other large carnivores, so Komodo dragons established themselves as the largest and strongest meat eaters. Young dragons eat mainly insects and smaller species of

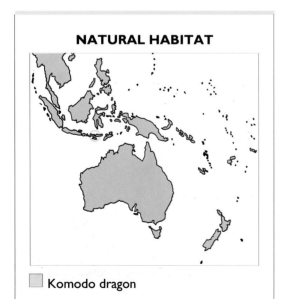

NATURAL HABITAT

☐ Komodo dragon

lizard. As they develop, they find larger and larger prey, going from rats and birds up to pigs and deer when fully grown. As well as hunting for live prey, they feed on the carcasses of dead animals. They are stealthy hunters, lurking in shrubs and bushes, and can move surprisingly fast when they need to on their short legs.

Maneating monsters?

If you came across a Komodo dragon in the wild, it would probably watch you with interest, just as you might watch it. It is unlikely that it would attack you, but if it came upon someone who had collapsed in a state of exhaustion, it would not hestitate to tear the body apart like a carcass. There have been reports of people being bitten by Komodo dragons and dying from their wounds.

Komodo dragons are voracious feeders. Two adult dragons often work together, gripping the meat in their teeth, digging their claws into the ground and jerking their heads backward in order to get at the flesh. If younger dragons threaten them, the adults snap at them and drive them away. Indeed, if adults are hungry, they seem to have no qualms about eating their young: examination of their feces has proved that they are cannibalistic.

Tongue testing

Like the other monitor lizards, Komodo dragons have long, spindly, forked tongues. They constantly flick their tongues out as though they are tasting the air. This idea is not far from the truth. These lizards use their tongues to draw air into their mouths toward the sensory organs in the roof of the mouth. These sense certain chemicals in the air: the animals are not tasting or smelling the chemicals, but the information is used by the dragon to find water or hunt for food.

Male Komodo dragons often fight for their rights during the breeding season. They rear up on their hind legs, with tails behind to steady themselves, and wrestle with each other until one falls over. The females bury the eggs in the ground and the young fend for themselves.

▼ *Komodo dragons have a lumbering walk, but can move rapidly if they need to. They are also capable of climbing trees or swimming in the sea.*

See also **Monitor**

Glossary

Abdomen

(in vertebrates) the part of the body that contains most of the digestive tract; (in insects and spiders) the rear part of the body, usually forming its bulk

Aquatic

living in water

Carnivore

any flesh-eating animal

Carrion

the decaying flesh of a dead animal

Defoliate

to strip trees and bushes of their leaves

Deforestation

the process of removing trees from an area – particularly rainforests

Display

a pattern of activity where a creature shows off to others, often associated with mating

Diurnal

active during the day
• see also nocturnal

Ecology

the relationship between a living organism and its environment

Fertilization

the penetration of the female egg by the male sperm in order to create offspring

Fledgling

a young bird that has grown its feathers

Gestation

the process of growth of an embryo inside a mammal's body – the gestation period is the duration of a pregnancy

Grassland

a large, usually flat tract of land with some scattered bushes but few trees. Grasslands have different names on different continents, including pampas, prairie, steppe and veldt

Habitat

the environment where a species is normally found

Herbivore

any plant-eating animal

Hibernate

to spend the winter season in a dormant or inactive state

Home range

the area normally traveled by an individual during its lifespan

Incubation

the time an embryo in an egg takes to develop before hatching; birds' eggs have to be kept warm for the incubation period

Insectivore

any insect-eating animal

Invertebrate

any animal that does not have a backbone

Marine

living in the sea

Metamorphosis

a change of form during the life cycle of a creature, from egg, through larva and pupa to adult

Migration

the process of moving from one area to another, usually with the change of season

Nestling

a young bird that has not yet learned to fly

Nocturnal

active at night

Nurse

to provide milk (from the mother's teats) for a baby mammal

Omnivore

a creature that eats both plants and animals

Parasite

a plant or animal that is dependent on another (known as the host) but does not give benefit to the host

Predator

any species that preys upon (hunts) other species

Prehensile

fingers, toes or a tail that can grip onto things

Range

the parts of the world in which a particular species is found

Roosting

sleeping (usually used to describe sleeping birds)

Spawn

to produce eggs in large quantities; used to describe the way fish, mollusks, coral, and amphibians lay eggs (often unfertilized) underwater

Symbiosis

a relationship between animals where each gains particular benefits from living close to the other; such animals are said to have a symbiotic relationship

Territory

the area occupied by a single animal or group of animals, to the exclusion of others of the same species; often defended by aggressive displays

Vertebrate

animal with a backbone